10662289

Neighbor

Neighbor

Christian Encounters with "Illegal" Immigration

BEN DANIEL

© 2010 Ben Daniel
foreword © 2010 Westminster John Knox Press

First edition
Published by Westminster John Knox Press
Louisville, Kentucky

10 11 12 13 14 15 16 17 18 19—10 9 8 7 6 5 4 3 2 1

All rights reserved. No part of this book may be reproduced or transmitted in any form or by any means, electronic or mechanical, including photocopying, recording, or by any information storage or retrieval system, without permission in writing from the publisher. For information, address Westminster John Knox Press, 100 Witherspoon Street, Louisville, Kentucky 40202-1396. Or contact us online at www.wjkbooks.com.

Book design by Sharon Adams
Cover design by designpointinc.com
Cover art: © iStockphoto.com. Note: The content is being used for illustrative purposes only; people depicted in the content are models.

Library of Congress Cataloging-in-Publication Data

Daniel, Ben.
Neighbor : Christian encounters with "illegal" immigration / Ben Daniel.—1st ed.
p. cm.
Includes index.
ISBN 978-0-664-23651-9 (alk. paper)
1. United States—Emigration and immigration—Religious aspects—Christianity.
2. Illegal aliens—United States. I. Title.
BR517.D26 2010
277.3'083086912—dc22

2010003670

PRINTED IN THE UNITED STATES OF AMERICA

♾ The paper used in this publication meets the minimum requirements of the American National Standard for Information Sciences—Permanence of Paper for Printed Library Materials, ANSI Z39.48-1992

Westminster John Knox Press advocates the responsible use of our natural resources. The text paper of this book is made from 30% post-consumer waste.

For Anne
with Love.

This simple act of falling in love is as beneficial as it is astonishing. It arrests the petrifying influence of years, disproves cold-blooded and cynical conclusions, and awakens dormant sensibilities.
—Robert Louis Stevenson

Contents

Foreword

This is an important book. It might just save the moral honor—not to mention the economic vibrancy—of our country. At the very least this book will forever strip away the ability of those who have raised their hands against immigrants to say that they are acting as Christians and patriots. Ben Daniel leaves us no room to hide anti-immigrant prejudice behind a fig leaf of piety.

When I was asked to write the foreword to this book, I wondered what I could possibly add. That was before I read it. What I didn't realize was what a deep personal chord this book would strike as soon as I opened it, and not just because it's poignant and well written. I had always thought about the "immigration issue" as a political matter. Until reading Ben's book, the question had never struck me on a personal level. Once I read the book, it made me recall my own family's history of immigration and being strangers in a foreign land.

My American parents moved to Europe in 1947 as missionaries to work with young people in the bombed-out cities following World War II. They settled in Switzerland (I was born there in 1952) because the railroads worked; Switzerland had avoided the carnage that befell the rest of the continent. Thus my parents were able to travel from Switzerland to Paris, Rotterdam, Milan, Amsterdam, and many other cities in Europe where they were conducting Bible studies and helping to start churches and youth groups.

Frank Schaeffer is author of *Patience with God—Faith for People Who Don't Like Religion (Or Atheism)*.

In 1954, having settled in the small Roman Catholic farming village of Champéry, my parents fell afoul of the local authorities who were (back then) strict anti-Protestant Roman Catholics. (Note: Switzerland is divided into cantons [states] that are designated as Roman Catholic or Protestant.) As evangelical missionaries, my parents were unwelcome. The local priest became suspicious of these outsiders and their potential religious influence in "his" village. He appealed to the local bishop who, in turn, went to the secular authorities. Our residency permits were canceled and we were thrown out of the Roman Catholic canton of Valais.

With no fixed address my penniless parents were reclassified as undocumented aliens and told to leave Switzerland, unless they could find another community that would issue residency permits within a matter of weeks. So it became imperative that they find another town in the Protestant part of Switzerland that would accept them. As a child of these missionaries—Francis and Edith Schaeffer, who founded the ministry of L'Abri Fellowship and then became well-known evangelical leaders—I grew up hearing our own "miraculous exodus story" of how my parents' prayers were answered and—just in the nick of time—a village council in the (Protestant) canton of Vaud allowed our family to settle, thus preventing us from being expelled.

Besides this bit of family lore, throughout my childhood I grew up surrounded by the migrant workers from Italy who (in those days) provided the "cheap labor" in Switzerland in the same way that so many Mexican migrants are the backbone of large sectors of the American economy today—hard-working people striving for low pay and with no rights who are resented by the very people who depend on their labor to maintain a high standard of living for themselves. I remember my father often speaking about how unjust he thought it was that the Italian laborers were treated as third-class human beings, and never allowed to bring their families with them when they were granted temporary work permits, lest they settle in Switzerland. The xenophobic Swiss wanted the fruits of the Italians' labors but not the Italians. Moreover, in my parents' ministry of L'Abri, their open door policy meant that from time to time some of our guests included refugees from what was then the communist bloc. Some even had scars to show a fascinated little boy (me!) that memorialized their daring escapes. So I grew up aware that the "good guys" were always on the side of the strangers in our midst, a view my parents reinforced with constant references to the biblical prophets.

I mention this snippet of personal history because reading this book reminded me about what it feels like to be an outsider. (Also, Ben includes a fascinating chapter about how John Calvin fought for immigrants' rights in reformed Geneva, Switzerland, so there's actually a Swiss connection here, besides my own family history.) Of course for us Schaeffers, compared to the emotional and economic uncertainties of today's immigrants in America, the stakes were low. We didn't face death in a desert, or grinding, life-threatening poverty. Nor did we face far right neo-Nazi vigilantes who have been known to murder immigrants in cold blood. Even so I feel a visceral connection to the stories herein and the whole question of sojourn as well as spiritual pilgrimage.

But here's the point: given my background, where I assumed that conservative Christianity was part and parcel of being open to and generous with immigrants, imagine my shock to learn that there were other people calling themselves Christians who somehow had missed the entire lesson of the Scriptures as to how we're to treat the stranger in our midst. In the United States, all too often the word *Christian* has come to signify right-wing bigotry. The same people who tell us that we need to police our borders with vigilantes and, if need be, shoot down would-be job seekers in cold blood to "protect America" are doing dreadful and un-Christ-like things in Jesus' name. How I wish they would take seriously the Christ-centered counter argument found in this book. When it comes to how we receive the stranger in our land, this book makes what I regard as a watertight case. The moving accounts here—including stories about churches that are helping immigrants being picketed by screaming fascists—lay out both the argument for, and the call to, conscience. This book presents a choice to anyone who follows Christ: *Do I believe in the moral teaching of my faith more than I believe in the constructs of humankind, nationalism, and borders*?

The wonderful thing about Ben Daniel's book is that it's one of those rare documents that could actually change minds. There are still enough Americans trying to live moral lives based on consistent Christian beliefs who may still be reached by biblical arguments that this book may well have a direct impact on American policy.

One thing is certain: it removes any excuse for those who would pursue an anti-immigrant policy while cloaking it in some sort of Christian mantle of respectability. Ben has stripped away that cloak, hopefully forever.

No one whose heart is the least susceptible to the power of God's love will be able to ignore the case made herein or the deeply moving stories told. This book calls us back to our better selves. It is also a call for American economic renewal, because the key to a prosperous future is not a frightened zero-sum xenophobic (much less racist) view of the human race but open borders, charity, love, freedom, and hope.

Frank Schaeffer

Acknowledgments

This book began at a Thai restaurant in San Francisco's Financial District when my friend and dining companion, Mark Tauber, suggested I write a book about the New Sanctuary Movement. Mark has been reading my writing and encouraging me as a writer since we were in college together. Mark is also the vice president and publisher at HarperOne, one of the world's largest publishers of religious books and is, therefore, someone whose ideas about which books should be written are worth listening to.

Mark introduced me to Mickey Maudlin, an editor at HarperOne, and to Mason Funk, a filmmaker from Los Angeles—both of whose ideas were invaluable in the early days of this book's development; later Mark helped this book find a home at Westminster John Knox Press. In many ways, Mark was this book's *coyote*, guiding it through a wilderness of uncertainty and finding it a safe home with an excellent publisher. I am deeply grateful to Jana Riess and the folks at Westminster John Knox for making this book come to life. I believe that the best writing happens when authors trust the decisions of their editors and follow their lead. Jana was very easy to trust and to follow.

Throughout the process of the book's development and writing, I leaned heavily upon the wisdom and experience of my father, John M. Daniel, who besides being supportive as a parent, was generous with his advice as a publisher, editor, and writer. For me it is a matter of great happiness that my father is a literary friend.

I am indebted to a great many folks who lent me advice and support as this book took shape and came together. A partial list of those who came to my aid during the writing of this book includes Frank Schaeffer, who was kind enough to write this book's foreword; my neighbors Francisco, Ariceli, Francisco, Jr., and Danny who introduced me to St. Toribio Romo; Mama Ruth and my godchildren in New Mexico who shared their hospitality and good cheer; Doug Learned, who encouraged me to cut the bull from one of my chapters; J. J. Chacon, who for years has provided me with a Web presence; the Rev. Carol Bean, who connected me to the Sanctuary Movement; Stan de Voogd, who put me in touch with Mark Adams and the folks at *Frontera de Cristo* (to whom I am also thankful); Kristen Henny Burt, who helped me establish connections in the schools; and Gene Hewitt, who assured me that it's good for a pastor to be a writer. I am thankful for the friendship and support of Tone the Bone and Jackie DeRose, who cheered me on as they listened to excerpts from early drafts of this book. I am thankful also for the sustenance of Craig Smith's soulful Scottish humor ¡Alba gu bràth, amigo! Most of all, I am grateful to all those kindhearted souls who let me interview them, thereby lending me their words for use in this book. This is an extraordinary gift.

I wrote this book in venues as geographically diverse as the public library in Sandwich, Massachusetts, the Glen Workshop in Santa Fe, New Mexico (an excellent event), and the Blue Mug Café in Escondido, California. But my best writing tended to happen at *Café do Canto* in San José's Little Portugal neighborhood. Thanks to Lee and Joe behind the counter and to the patrons—especially Maria and Frank—who have become a community for me.

When I'm not writing books I am a Presbyterian minister, and I am grateful to the congregation, session, and staff of Foothill Presbyterian Church in San José, California for their support.

My parents, Karen and Michael Moreland, gave me the gift of a childhood nurtured in an open-minded, compassionate faith, for which I am eternally grateful, and they supported me and cheered me on while I wrote this book.

My children, Mimi, Nellie, William, and my foster daughter, Kate, have endured the absence and occasional spaciness of a dad writing a book while holding down a full-time job. They're good sports.

And my wife, Anne Marie, fills my life with beauty. As my primary reader she makes me a better writer, and as a woman she makes me a better man.

Thank you.

Introduction

Immigration Reconsidered

"So. What do you know about immigration?"

It's a question I heard often as I wrote this book, and I've had the opportunity to try out a range of responses. At first I answered the question biographically. I am the pastor of a congregation whose two hundred members come from more than twenty different countries and grew up speaking at least that many different languages. For seven years I served on the fundraising board of Presbyterian Border Ministry, a binational organization supported by the Presbyterian Church (U.S.A.) and the National Presbyterian Church of Mexico. Two of my three children are immigrants, as is my foster daughter. I now live across the street from Our Lady of Guadalupe Catholic Church in a neighborhood in San José, California that is peopled almost entirely by immigrants. In fact, I have lived either across the street from, next door to, or in the same house as immigrants since I was a senior in college.

So I have some personal experience with immigration that has been augmented by a good bit of study and research, but as the writing of this book progressed, my personal experience with immigrants and my knowledge of the issues stopped being the driving force behind my writing. What became paramount in writing a book on how American Christians respond to undocumented migration is the knowledge that my book will help its readers confront a set of common misconceptions and prejudices, born of ignorance and xenophobia, that are pervasive in the United States today and that drive the national debate around immigration.

Then I started interviewing people whose lives were directly affected by the realities of United States' immigration policy. I spoke with a wide range of people, from a member of Congress to a woman who lives under the constant threat of deportation and is receiving sanctuary in a southern California church. I came to see that whatever I may or may not know about immigration, and whatever my motivation for writing about immigration, by writing about immigration I was writing about people, and I was addressing the question once asked of Jesus: "Who is my neighbor?"

According to the Gospel of Luke, a lawyer asked Jesus what was required to inherit eternal life. Jesus replied by asking the legal expert what his own tradition required. He responded by quoting from the Torah: "You shall love the Lord your God with all your heart, and with all your soul, and with all your strength, and with all your mind; and your neighbor as yourself" (Luke 10:27).

Jesus was satisfied with this answer, but the lawyer wanted to justify himself, so he asked Jesus the question that inspired the title of this book: "Who is my neighbor?"

In response, Jesus told a parable, known popularly as "The Good Samaritan":

> A man was going down from Jerusalem to Jericho, and fell into the hands of robbers, who stripped him, beat him, and went away, leaving him half dead. Now by chance a priest was going down that road; and when he saw him, he passed by on the other side. So likewise a Levite, when he came to the place and saw him, passed by on the other side. But a Samaritan while traveling came near him; and when he saw him, he was moved with pity. He went to him and bandaged his wounds, having poured oil and wine on them. Then he put him on his own animal, brought him to an inn, and took care of him. The next day he took out two denarii, gave them to the innkeeper, and said, "Take care of him; and when I come back, I will repay you whatever more you spend." (Luke 10:30–36)

Jesus then asked the lawyer, "Which of these three do you think was a neighbor to the man who fell into the hands of the robbers?" And the answer was easy. It was the merciful Samaritan. "Go and do likewise," said Jesus (Luke 10:36–37).

"Go and do likewise" is the main message many readers take from the parable of the Good Samaritan, and it's a good message. Certainly the Good Samaritan is a biblical character worthy of emulation, but "go and do likewise" is not the answer to the question that prompted Jesus to tell the parable in the first place.

Jesus told the parable in response to the question, "Who is this person—the one I am supposed to 'love as myself'—who is my neighbor?" In the parable, Jesus answers the question by inviting his followers to imagine they are like a traveler who has been beaten up, left for dead, and ignored by the religious establishment; the neighbor to be loved (and imitated) is the Samaritan, a foreigner who is the victim of ancient prejudice and xenophobia, who looks past long-held mutual animosity and saves the life of a man who had been beaten within an inch of his life.

So in the context of a discussion around illegal immigration, when we ask "who is my neighbor?" the answer is not so much a person who may benefit from our charity (though charity is good and often needed) or from a change in public policy (something we also need), but rather the person from outside our community who saves and blesses us despite the walls erected by long-held hostility.

Here is what I have found: those who practice Christian hospitality by welcoming outsiders—not just as guests to be endured, but as neighbors, as true and valued members of the community—usually are blessed by those newcomers. Their lives are enriched. My desire for this book, then, is not so much that it will inspire charity or political activism (though I do not wish to discourage either), but that readers will recognize in undocumented immigrants the potential for long-lasting, life-giving friendship.

"Do you believe in open borders?"

This has been the second-most frequent question I've encountered over the course of writing this book. For the most part, I've tried to dodge that question, because this is a book about people rather than policy. Nonetheless, questions of policy really cannot be ignored when we talk about immigration. I have little doubt that my opinions and inclinations will be evident to anyone who reads this book, but it seems fair for me to state my opinions plainly up front. Here, then, are five changes that I feel must be included in any just reform of American immigration policy.

1. The United States Government must provide visas for seasonal work, particularly for those working in the agricultural sector. Issuing visas for seasonal work would likely have the effect of decreasing the number of immigrants from Mexico living permanently in the United States because with visas workers could return to Mexico at the end of each season and not feel compelled to move their families north.
2. Families should be kept together. Current laws that separate mixed-status spouses or that deport parents, separating them from their children, should be changed. When parents are deported, leaving citizen children without a mother or a father, no one benefits.
3. Children brought across the border by their parents should be treated differently than adults who immigrated alone, even after those children are adults. Under current immigration law, adults who came to the United States as children are treated exactly as if they themselves had made the decision to immigrate. If they lack documentation, they live under the constant threat of deportation, and in many states they are denied driver's licenses, seriously hampering their chances of finding meaningful work. Even if they are legal residents, they face the possibility of deportation, even for relatively minor offenses.
4. If I could do so with any kind of efficacy, I'd stand by the fence that now runs along the border from the Pacific Ocean to the Rio Grande, and I'd declare with every possible ounce of conviction, "Mr. Obama, tear down this wall!" The border fence is a ridiculous waste of money and, often, a tragic waste of human life. The wall doesn't keep people out of the United States; it just encourages people to cross the border in increasingly dangerous places. Besides, as expensive as walls and fences are to build and maintain, ladders are cheap. The only people who benefit from the wall are politicians whose constituents like easy answers to complex issues.
5. I firmly believe that the movement of goods and services across the border should be controlled. Duty fees must be collected and contraband must be stopped, but the best way to control the flow of people is with economic development south of the border and with enforcement north of the border that targets businesses that hire undocumented persons rather than the migrants themselves.

My opinions are not unique to the progressive community in the United States, nor are they original to me. I heard variations on these themes everywhere I went in the United States and Mexico researching this book. This is not to say that everyone in the United States and Mexico agrees with me—not even close—but when discussions around immigration are educated, thoughtful, and separated from fear, prejudice, and xenophobia, consensus starts to appear.

The book you are reading is written in three parts. The first part begins with a ghost story and seeks to make a theological, biblical, historical, and reasonable argument that the Christian faith is, at its core, a religion that is by and for immigrants. In the second part I address immigration policy by interviewing Rep. Zoe Lofgren (D-CA), chair of the subcommittee responsible for writing immigration reform legislation in the United States House of Representatives, and Judge Robert Brack, a federal judge in Los Cruces, New Mexico, who is responsible for enforcing our nation's immigration policy. In the third part of the book, I tell stories of American Christians interacting with immigrants in ways that are creative, positive, and faithful. After each part of the book I have included brief sections for reflection and action that can be used in church discussion groups or for individual study. These sections are meant to inspire thoughtfulness and include questions that will inspire discussion and debate.

When you have finished the book you now have in your hands, my prayer is not so much that you will agree with me, but that you will find yourself blessed by the stories of the neighbors you will meet in these pages, for indeed they have been a blessing to me, and it is my pleasure to share this blessing with you.

Ben Daniel,
Writing from *Café do Canto*
Little Portugal
San José, California
August, 2009

Part 1

In The Spirit of Toribio Romo

Chapter 1

Father Toribio's Ghost

> *I would rather live in a world where my life is surrounded by mystery than live in a world so small that my mind could comprehend it.*
>
> *—Harry Emerson Fosdick*

Some years ago, I was standing outside my condominium in East San José, watching my children play with some neighbor kids and I noticed something odd. One of my children's playmates was wearing a T-shirt printed with the image of a young man in a clerical collar. As someone who, from time to time, wears a clerical collar to work, I am acutely aware of how un-cool they are. Most people who end up on T-shirts are cool. If a guy wears a football jersey to work, you expect him to be on a T-shirt because football players are cool, as are firefighters, race-car drivers, and Hannah Montana. But a man of the cloth? Not so much.

The mother of the kid in the preacher T-shirt was outside, as was the mother of another of the young children. I asked about the shirt. "That's Toribio Romo," said the mom who dressed her boy in the shirt that made my profession look cooler than it actually is. She mentioned Toribio Romo's name as if she expected me to be familiar with him. When she saw that I had no idea who she was talking about, she explained, "He's a saint from my husband's hometown. Migrants pray to him before crossing the desert."

Turning to the other mother, she asked, "Did you pray to Toribio when you came north?"

"No," came the reply, "I prayed to the virgin of San Juan." She fished a card out of her purse. On one side was a painting of the mother of Jesus as an infant, and on the other was a prayer to the baby-faced Queen of Heaven. "But when I go back next summer I will visit Toribio's shrine. He has helped a lot of people."

In that moment I realized that as much as Americans love to argue and debate about immigration—particularly undocumented migration—most of us, as we shout out our opinions, are overlooking something important: immigration is not just about economics and politics. Immigration is also a religious phenomenon. For many immigrants, particularly those from Mexico, migration is a physical journey through a spiritual landscape marked with deep faith and peopled, as often as not, with angels, demons, and a crowd of folk saints, and motivated by a sense of divine purpose.

It seems possible that the issues surrounding undocumented immigration cannot fully be grasped without understanding that many immigrants, especially those who have entered the United States with neither papers nor permission, are not just economically motivated wayfarers. They are latter-day pilgrims.

When we think of immigrants as pilgrims—as spiritual travelers—most Americans call to mind the English who crossed the Atlantic Ocean on the *Mayflower*, seeking a life free from the religious persecutions of England. These are the folks who ate turkey with the local Indians and established Thanksgiving, the guys with buckled shoes and oddly-shaped hats, people who are rumored to have lain awake at night, worrying that someone, somewhere, was having fun.

Seldom, however, do we use the word "pilgrim" to describe latter-day immigrants who cross the Sonora Desert or ford the Rio Grande, enduring the dangers of heat and hunger and exhaustion, evading border patrols and vigilante civilians to find a life of economic viability in *El Norte*.

Pilgrims, to the American mind, do not bus tables in Topeka or harvest lettuce in California's Salinas Valley, yet for many undocumented immigrants the trip across the frontier between the United States and Mexico becomes a pilgrimage. Even when the migrants' reasons for leaving home are secular, born of economic necessity perhaps or inspired by a longing for adventure, the epic nature of such migrations—overland on overcrowded buses, through the desert on foot, and into a strange and foreign landscape—often inspires a quickening of faith and an attentiveness to matters of the spirit.

Such faith-based language for the journey of immigration appeals to the Bible's frequent use of immigration as a metaphor for human spiritual journeys, but it also has roots deep within the soil of the grass-roots religion and populist spiritual expressions that are common in Mexico and points south.

This spiritual renewal born of the immigrant experience is especially evident in the growing devotion to the man on my neighbor's shirt, St. Toribio Romo González,[1] a martyred Catholic priest born in Santa Ana de Guadalupe, a small village in the Mexican state of Jalisco, a region known for its excellent tequila if not, necessarily, for its sainted clergymen.

Santa Ana de Guadalupe is a village like many in Mexico. It is poor, limited in resources and in economic opportunities. It is the kind of place that easily could be missed, a place that many people in Mexico have felt compelled to leave, searching for manufacturing jobs in the NAFTA boom towns of the U.S./Mexico border, or in the United States—if by luck or resourcefulness they are able to cross the border.

Or, perhaps they will cross the Sonora Desert or ford the *Rio Bravo*[2] with the help of Father Toribio's ghost.

Technically, I'm not sure that an oft-repeated, unverifiable story of unknown authorship can be called an "urban legend" if it starts out in the desert along the U.S./Mexico border, but reports of Father Toribio Romo's ghost almost always are the same:

> I was crossing the border and became separated from my group. I was tired and thirsty. My feet were blistered and I could barely walk. It was dusk and I was cold. In my despair I collapsed, giving up my spirit. Suddenly I was approached by a young priest. He had blue eyes and he spoke perfect Spanish. He gave me water and food and bandages for my feet. He handed me some money and showed me the quickest way to the nearest town, where, he assured me, there would be a job waiting for me. As we parted I asked him how I ever could repay him.
>
> "Don't worry about repaying me," he said, "but when you return to Mexico, come visit me in Santa Ana de Guadalupe in Jalisco. My name is Toribio Romo."

> I followed the young priest's directions. I found a job and made a good life for myself in El Norte.
>
> When I returned to visit my family in Mexico, I kept my promise. I drove from my home in Sinaloa to Jalisco, to Santa Ana de Guadalupe. It's a small village, and I assumed that everyone would know the young priest who saved my life. When I asked after Toribio Romo, the villagers directed me to a local church. Upon entering, I found myself looking at a photo of the same priest who had come to my aid; only here in the church at Santa Ana de Guadalupe did I learn that he had been dead for many years.

Hundreds of such testimonies are written out and displayed in Santa Ana de Guadalupe's hilltop chapel, an edifice that Toribio Romo helped to design and build, and from whose altar the future saint said his first mass.[3]

Toribio Romo is an honest-to-goodness saint, which is to say that, unlike most Mexican folk saints, the Vatican recognizes him as such. Born in 1900 in a small farmhouse outside of Santa Ana, Toribio entered seminary as a young teenager and was ordained at the age of 21. He served several churches in the Jalisco highlands; he was pious, dedicated to children; and he displayed a keen interest in organizing labor unions. He was a good priest, leading a fairly unremarkable existence until the history of his troubled homeland changed his life.

In Mexico, the relationship between church and state always has been strained, but it reached a low point during the first half of the twentieth century. In 1917, after the end of a long and bloody civil war, a new Mexican constitution outlawed monastic orders, forbade religious education in schools, barred clergy from voting, and prevented religious institutions from owning property. At first, the government's enforcement of harsher elements within the constitution was limited, but in June 1926, the newly elected Mexican president, Plutarco Elías Calles, issued an executive order meant to enforce the anticlerical provisions of the constitution. The laws imposed by Calles went further than the constitution, outlawing the use of clerical garb by priests, imposing a five-year prison sentence upon priests who criticized the Mexican government, and forbidding worship outside of church buildings.

In Jalisco, where piety remained strong, Catholics resisted the secularizing forces of the Mexican government—in the name of the

Virgin of Guadalupe and Christ the King—by waging a bloody civil war. Known as the "Cristero War," the conflict lasted between 1926 and 1929 and claimed more than 90,000 lives.

Though he never took up arms, Father Romo was an ardent supporter of the Cristero cause. In the months leading up to the Mexican government's crackdown on Catholicism, Toribio Romo celebrated an outdoor mass at which 15,000 faithful are reported to have joined their voices in what eventually would become the rallying cry of the Cristero War: "*¡Viva Cristo Rey!*" Long live Christ the King![4]

This, of course, made Toribio Romo a criminal under Mexican law. On Ash Wednesday in 1928, after evading the authorities for nearly a year and a half, the future saint went into hiding in the city of Tequila, where he was serving as a parish priest. Three days later, members of a local militia found and shot him during his siesta (his last words, unremarkably, were, "Yes, I'm Toribio Romo. Don't kill me!"). Recognizing his martyrdom, Pope John Paul II canonized Father Toribio Romo in 2000 along with 24 other martyrs of the Cristero War.

Almost immediately after his assassination, the people of Santa Ana de Guadalupe began to venerate Toribio Romo, but until 2000 they did so without the Vatican's blessing and his name was not well known outside of the Jalisco highlands. All that has changed since reports of Father Toribio's benevolent ghost began to appear sometime in the 1970s, and now that the Vatican officially has endorsed him, St. Toribio's following is getting larger. Well north of the Mexican border, fans of Toribio Romo can purchase his likeness printed on T-shirts and votive candles, key chains and other religious trinkets; though the Vatican has yet to endorse him as such, many Catholics in the United States and Mexico consider St. Toribio Romo to be the patron of undocumented migrants.

The growing popularity of St. Toribio Romo has transformed Santa Ana de Guadalupe. In recent years, pilgrims and tourists have arrived by the busload to climb the hill upon which Toribio Romo's church stands, and to gaze with reverence upon the relics contained therein: the ossuary that holds Father Romo's bones, the clothes he was wearing on the day he became a martyr, and a little vial of blood, drawn from his body just minutes after his death.

Hundreds of miles to the north of Santa Ana de Guadalupe, in Altar, a slightly larger and dustier town in the Sonora Desert, devotion to

Toribio Romo is fervent. As the United States has continued to fortify the border, building walls and escalating the numbers of border patrol agents in populated areas, those who cross into the United States on foot increasingly have wandered further into the Sonora Desert, and the village of Altar has become the last stop before the desert-crossing into Arizona. Each day, dozens of buses ferry migrants from Altar to the border. Often, Mexican officials stop the buses in an attempt to dissuade those prepared to make the journey and, failing to do so, give advice and warnings to those determined to go on.

As they do in Santa Ana de Guadalupe, vendors in Altar sell trinkets and tokens decorated with Toribio's image. Father Romo's statue has a place of prominence in Altar's plaza, and each day, those journeying to the north pay their respects with prayers such as,

> Te suplicamos, señor que por intercesión de la Santísima Virgen y Santo Toribio Romo González nuestro hermano mexicano que tanto se preocupó en vida por los migrantes y ahora a alcanzado de ti, milagros en nuestro favor, que nos ayude en nuestras necesidades. A tí, Santo Toribio, encomendamos nuestra peregrinación por estas lejanas tierras, para alcanzar el fin por el que hemos dejado nuestras familias, pidiendote la protección para nosotros y para esos pedazos de corazón que dejamos en casa. Que nuestros afanes sirven para ganar tanto lo material para vivir mejor, como la gracia para alcanzar el cielo.
>
> Cuida nuestra fe. Que por ningún motivo nos dejamos engañar por falsas doctrinas. Que tomemos por ejemplo y creamos, como tu hasta la muerte, diciendo: ¡Viva Cristo Rey y Santa María Guadalupe!, así sea.
>
> (Lord, we make supplication to you by the intercession of the Holy Virgin and St. Toribio Romo González, our Mexican brother who showed concern for immigrants in life and now, having reached your side, has worked miracles in our favor, helping us meet our needs. To you, St. Toribio, we commend our pilgrimage to far-off lands to reach, at last, the reasons for which we left our families, asking your protection for us and for these pieces of our hearts which we have left at home. May our efforts serve to gain the material needs to live a better life and the grace to reach you in heaven.
>
> Guard our faith. May we be kept from being entangled in false doctrines. May we take your example, believing unto death and,

like you, saying "long live Christ the King, and Saint Mary of Guadalupe! Amen.)[5]

The reported benevolence of Father Toribio's ghost raises important questions for North American Christians: might God look with favor upon the prayers of those who seek to enter the United States without permission? Would God provide a patron saint to aid illegal immigrants in their journey to the United States? Is it possible for heaven to look favorably upon those who break laws of the United States to find employment on U.S. soil? Might divine protection extend to men and women, boys and girls, deemed to be illegal sojourners in the land of the free?

To those who have come into the United States in search of opportunities unavailable to them at home, the answer usually is yes. There is an overwhelming and growing sense among undocumented immigrants that their journeys are blessed by God—often through the intercession of saints such as Toribio Romo—and the knowledge that they have arrived in the United States by the grace of God has helped to instill a particularly strong faith among many of America's undocumented Christians.[6]

This distinctly immigrant spirituality is strongly dependent upon the Bible's witness to a God with an affinity for those who live as sojourners in foreign lands.

Our Lady of Guadalupe Roman Catholic Church in San José, California is a congregation with a significant population of undocumented immigrants from Mexico. Toribio Romo's portrait hangs in the church's prayer chapel. When I asked about devotion to Toribio Romo, a lay leader in the parish who works at the church's bookstore on weekends told me that the bookshop is doing a lot of business selling objects of devotion that feature Toribio Romo. "They come in and they say to me, 'This is the saint who brought me across.'"

At the church's bookshop I picked up a booklet outlining a novena[7]—a nine-day cycle of prayers—in honor of St. Toribio. For each day there is a Scripture reading, a story from the life of Father Toribio, and directions for prayer. It is full of this immigrant spirituality.

As a way of remembering and honoring St. Toribio Romo's priestly vocation, the novena's first day begins with words from the book of Genesis:

> Now the LORD said to Abram, "Go from your country and your kindred and your father's house to the land that I will show you. I will make you a great nation, and I will bless you, and make your name great, so that you will be a blessing. (Gen. 12:1–2)

The novena's fourth day is meant to remember Toribio Romo's charitable work and to inspire the faithful to similar social action. The reading is from 1 Peter,

> Beloved, I urge you as aliens and exiles to abstain from the desires of the flesh that wage war against the soul. Conduct yourselves honorably among the Gentiles, so that, though they malign you as evildoers, they may see your honorable deeds and glorify God when he comes to judge. (1 Pet. 2:11–12)

The novena chooses Scripture passages that reflect an immigrant spirituality. Few American Protestants would look to the call of Abram when looking for Scriptures that talk about a priestly vocation, and even fewer would consider their status as "aliens and exiles" as a pretext for social action, but this is a salient feature of the immigrant spirit.

Brother[8] Bill Minkel is a Franciscan priest on the pastoral staff of the aforementioned Our Lady of Guadalupe Catholic Church in San José. I took him to lunch and asked him about Toribio Romo and the spirituality of immigration. "Salvation comes through the poor," he told me. "The devotion is palpable. Their prayers, their commitment to family, their hospitality, and kindness all demonstrate a faithfulness that energized me. It's why I wanted to work at Our Lady of Guadalupe. I wanted to be near to the salvation that is so present in the life of my congregation."

Before entering the Franciscan order, Brother Bill worked for more than twenty years as a police officer in San Francisco, where he first encountered God alive among the poor in some of the city's rougher neighborhoods. Because he has a background in law enforcement, I asked him about the fact that so many of his parishioners come to the United States in violation of American law. "Jesus healed on the Sabbath," he reminded me. "In those days it was against the law to heal on the Sabbath, and for the most part, laws meant to keep the

Sabbath holy were good laws, laws that benefited society. Sometimes you have to follow a higher law."

There is no question that the U.S./Mexico border, where migrants report being aided by Toribio Romo, is a place where certain segments of the population follow laws intermittently and where law enforcement operates with limited efficacy. The frontier is long, dusty, and inhospitable, alternating between barren desert and immense NAFTA boomtowns such as Juarez and Tijuana. It is a landscape that calls to mind both the wild west of American myth, and also the gangland neighborhoods of America's contemporary urban wastelands. Outlaw gangs terrorize local populations on both sides of the border. Most of the criminals along the border smuggle narcotics to satisfy the insatiable American appetite for drugs, but many also deal in human traffic and other contraband.

Since the 1990s, a new musical genre, *narcocorrido*, celebrates the lawlessness of the border region. Though the music features the accordion pulsating to a polka beat—a *norteño* sound that was borrowed from the Bohemian immigrants who settled the Rio Grande valley in the years before Texas became the twenty-eighth state—*narcocorrido* is an awful lot like gangsta rap. Both musical genres celebrate the violence and transient wealth of the drug trade. Both kinds of music are accused of contributing to the delinquency of their fan base. Denizens of both *narcocorrido* and gangsta rap seem to draw enjoyment from playing their favorite tunes as loudly as possible while waiting for traffic lights to turn green; critics of both genres say that the music all sounds the same from one song to the next.

One of the bright stars in the *narcocorrido* constellation is *Los Originales de San Juan*, a band from Fresno, California, which has sold more than four million albums in the last decade. In 2007, *Los Originales* released an album—their twenty-fifth—called *Ojalá que la Vida me Alcance* ("O to Achieve a Full Life"). Most of the album's tracks are standard *narcocorrido* fare: celebrations of a life spent in pursuit of the big rock candy mountain, ducking the law while in the employ of cruel drug bosses. There are a couple of songs about life behind bars. There are lots of guns involved; properly pimped pickup trucks are venerated; women are objectified.

Except for one track.

Folded into the mix of bad-guy ballads is "Santo Toribio Romo," an unexpected hymn to Father Toribio Romo that tells the story of his life and martyrdom. The song celebrates his angelic work of rescue and succor. The bridge is a prayer to Toribio Romo:

> Te pidimos que intercedes por nosotros
> Con nuestra Virgencita de Guadalupe,
> La patrona de todos los Mexicanos.
> (We ask that you intercede for us
> With the dear Virgin of Guadalupe,
> The patroness of every Mexican.)

That the immigrant spirituality embodied by devotion to Toribio Romo is as evident in the lyrics of a *narcocorrido* band as it is among the congregation at Our Lady of Guadalupe and in an officially sanctioned novena speaks to its broad appeal within the community of Mexican immigrants living in the United States. Surely it is a spiritual movement to be taken seriously.

After lunch I walked Brother Bill back to his office at Our Lady of Guadalupe. As we walked, Brother Bill waved to a member of his church whom we passed on the street. "There's a tough story," he told me. "That woman's husband is undocumented, which means he cannot get a driver's license, which means he cannot own a car. So he bought a truck and registered it in a friend's name. He was pulled over for a traffic violation, and when they found him to be driving without a license in a car he didn't own, they impounded the truck and fined his friend. It's tough. He needs that truck for work."

"This is why I'm encouraging a devotion to Toribio Romo," he told me. "We need all the help we can get."

And whatever a person may think about the possibility that the specter of a long-deceased priest may be working as a *santo pollero*, a holy coyote, a sainted smuggler of persons, leading God's children through the Sonora wilderness, it's worth asking if God is walking alongside those who immigrate to the United States. If God is walking with immigrants as they ford the Rio Grande, if God accompanies undocumented folks through the fiery heat of the desert, then perhaps American Christians need to walk with immigrants as well—not just to influence public policy, but to strengthen our faith and to deepen our spiritual connection to the Divine.

Chapter 2

Immigration as a Biblical Journey

[The Bible is] the "ultimate immigration handbook."
—Samuel Kobia, General Secretary of the World Council of Churches[1]

However hard it may be for Protestants living in a scientific age to believe the stories of Father Toribio's spectral ministrations to migrants wandering in the desert, the reputation of the saint from Tequila is entirely in keeping with the spirit of the Bible, which, in many ways, is a book about immigration. Walking alongside immigrants in the spiritual journey of migration has given me a deeper connection to the God I have met in the pages of the Bible and through my practice of rational, American Protestantism.

For the most part, my own walk alongside immigrants who have embarked upon a pilgrim's journey across the United States' southern border has been nongeographical—made of friendship, action, and solidarity. Sometimes, however, the journey has been one of actual footsteps.

On May 6, 2006, I was part of a group of local clergy who led a demonstration march through the streets of San José, California—from the working-class Latino neighborhood where I live to downtown San José, the heart of Silicon Valley's gleaming, high-rent, cosmopolitan urban core.

The U.S. Senate was debating HR4437, the so-called "Border Protection, Antiterrorism, and Illegal Immigration Control Act of

2005," a bill that would have made undocumented migration into the United States a felony, and would have made felons of anyone assisting migrants in any way.

In San José, 120,000 protestors marched that day. It was the largest demonstration in the history of my city and one of the biggest rallies among the many that were held around the country that weekend.

At the conclusion of the march we gathered in a park for speeches and music. I led the crowd in prayer and then stood shoulder to shoulder with a Conservative rabbi, a leader from Silicon Valley's sizable Sikh community, a Lutheran pastor, and a Catholic priest. Together we sang *De Colores* and raised our fists and chanted, "*Sí, se puede*," or "Yes, we can." It's the rallying cry of the United Farm Worker's Union, whose founder, Cesar Chavez, was a child of the San José neighborhood where the march began.

It was not, perhaps, the most likely place for someone like me to end up. I am a child of California's rural North Coast. In the demographics of my childhood there was a polarity between countercultural types who moved north from the Bay Area to be close to the land, and the older and more established community of folks historically connected to the timber industry, but I knew few people who were not just as white as I am. While things have changed since then, in the days of my childhood almost no one from south of the border had found their way behind the Redwood Curtain and into the community where I lived.

Nonetheless, I have become deeply involved in immigration issues. I had a conversion of sorts and, like most conversions, the change in my life that caused me to walk in close proximity to the pilgrim path of immigrants from Mexico and Central America was a process whose beginning is hard to recall but which had a definite moment of commitment born of a personal crisis. For me, the crisis came in the form of a handgun pointed in my general direction.

I am a graduate of Westmont College, an evangelical liberal arts college nestled in the beautiful mountains behind Santa Barbara, California. It is a good school that provided me with the opportunity to attend an urban studies program in San Francisco. While living in the college's residence in Pacific Heights (one of the City's posh neighborhoods) I commuted three times a week to the Mission District (one of the City's poor and predominantly Hispanic neighborhoods) to work with refugees from Central America—almost all of whom were in the United States illegally—at an Episcopal ministry called the Good Samaritan Center.

One of my jobs at the Good Samaritan Center was to help undocumented immigrants find employment and then to work with the employers to make sure they treated our clients well and paid them a decent wage. This is a responsibility I took on blithely, failing, at first, to comprehend that people tend to hire undocumented immigrants precisely *because* they don't want to treat them well or provide them with a decent wage.

So it was that at the ripe age of nineteen I found myself at a car wash in south San Francisco asking the establishment's proprietor to pay several hundred dollars of back pay owed to a Mayan refugee from Guatemala's bloody and protracted civil war. The man had been squirting, soaping, and buffing cars, unpaid, for a month. The owner of the car wash was a small man with the look of someone hardened by a lifetime spent in the inner city; I had the cockiness of a college student, the eloquence of a future preacher and (so I thought) the full moral weight of the Anglican Communion behind me. Given what I assumed was the superiority of my position, I fully expected to walk away from the car wash with an apology and a pocketful of my client's wages.

My opponent, however, had a gun. Game, set, and match to the bad guys.

The unpaid Guatemalan worker and I slouched back to the Center. He caught a bus to his other job (which also didn't pay him), and I crossed the street where I sat on a semifunctional swing set in a decrepit playground and tried not to hyperventilate.

What I realized at that moment was that I would be walking with immigrants for the rest of my life; and that is what has happened. Since graduating from seminary in 1993, I have not lived in a community or neighborhood without an immigrant majority. As I mentioned in the opening pages, I serve a congregation of 210 members who were born in more than twenty different countries. Two of my three children and my foster daughter are immigrants.

Immigration in the Old Testament/Hebrew Bible

Walking alongside immigrants I have discovered a deep spirituality that is rooted in the Biblical tradition. The Bible, it turns out, can be read as a tapestry woven of immigration stories and immigration-related themes. Most of the Bible came into its present form through the work of authors and editors who were immigrants—usually exiles and refugees—in search of spiritual and theological language to talk about what it means to live as strangers in a strange land.

The books of the Jewish Bible—the part of the Bible that Christians call the "Old Testament"—were chosen and set aside as Holy Writ by the rabbis of Jamnia following the destruction of Jerusalem's temple. After the Roman army sacked Jerusalem in 70 CE, the village of Jamnia, or *Yavneh*, became the authoritative center of Jewish learning. While Jamnia is not far from Jerusalem—it is situated near the Mediterranean coast in what was once Philistine territory and today is the Gaza Strip—the move to Jamnia represented a significant spiritual exile for the Jews. It was a migration from the City of God to a more secular hinterland.[2]

Over the course of six decades, the rabbis of Jamnia did the critically important work of reimagining Judaism without a temple. They formalized and standardized the practice of Jewish faithfulness without a priestly class and without rites such as animal sacrifice, which can happen only in a temple. They also did the work of deciding which books would be included in the Jewish Bible.

As a people living in exile, the rabbis of Jamnia sanctified as Scripture a collection of books and writings with a strong immigrant spirituality. Much of the Biblical writing embraced[3] at Jamnia comes from a prior exilic period of Jewish history when, after the destruction of Jerusalem's first temple, much of the Jewish population was living in exile in Babylon. Given this cultural context, it's not surprising that the Jewish scholars and religious leaders who compiled and edited most of the corpus of books that now comprise the Jewish Bible and the Christian Old Testament chose writings and oral traditions about an immigrant people who, after a period of nomadic existence and, later, slavery, left a land of torment and oppression and forged a new life together in a land of promise. To these stories of ancient immigration they added poetic and prophetic writings that often spoke words of comfort and promise to their context as immigrants living in exile.

Immigration is a theme that appears in the Bible's earliest chapters. Just three chapters in, as punishment for disobedience, the Creator exiles the first man and woman from the garden paradise in which they'd been placed. The story of the fall and expulsion from Eden is followed in rapid succession by a series of immigration stories in which the people favored by God are perpetual migrants and in which God invariably takes the side of the immigrant over and against the local, more established populations.

After the story of the first human migration out of Eden comes the account of the first murder—an act of fratricide. In the tale, the two sons born to the first man and woman make sacrifices to God, and the sacrifices of the younger son, Abel—a nomadic herder—are favored over those of his brother Cain, who is an agrarian settler. After he kills his brother in a fit of envious rage, Cain finds redemption (divine protection from would-be assailants) in God's punishment, as he is cursed to become a wanderer, a migrant, like his brother once had been.

The story of Cain and Abel precedes the narrative of the great flood, when God destroys most of creation in an effort to limit the spread of human sin. In the process of destruction and re-creation, God instructs Noah and his children to become migrants, to build an ark upon which God will transport them from the valley of Mesopotamia in modern-day Iraq to the mountains of Ararat where the modern states of Turkey, Iran, and Armenia meet.

As the biblical story unfolds, the righteousness restored in the immigration of Noah and his family is compromised once more with the establishment of a city, the notorious Babel, whose population attempts to build a tower as high as the heavens. In response to this arrogance, God punishes the citizens of Babel by confusing human language.

> And the LORD said, "Look, they are one people, and they have all one language; and this is only the beginning of what they will do; nothing that they propose to do will now be impossible for them. Come, let us go down, and confuse their language there, so that they will not understand one another's speech." So the LORD

> scattered them abroad from there over the face of all the earth, and they left off building the city. Therefore it was called Babel, because there the LORD confused the language of all the earth; and from there the LORD scattered them abroad over the face of all the earth. (Gen. 11:6–11)

This establishment of cultural diversity saves humanity from its pride and sends the people of the world, once more, into restorative migration.

The attention of the biblical story then turns to the history of the Hebrew people with the call of Abram and Sarai (later known as Abraham and Sarah), who, being obedient to God's calling, embark on a life of migration that led them from the city of Ur (near modern-day Baghdad), through Canaan (modern-day Israel and the occupied Palestinian territories), into Egypt, and eventually back into Canaan, where they settled in Hebron, a city in what today is the Occupied West Bank.

For three generations the family of Abraham lives in Canaan as immigrants. They do not adopt the language or culture of the local populace; instead, they continue to worship the God who had called them to the pilgrimage path of an immigrant life. When it comes time for their sons and heirs to marry, they send them back to Mesopotamia to find wives from the "old country."

In perhaps the most gripping and compelling of the Bible's immigrant narratives, Abraham's great-grandson, Joseph, who is kidnapped by jealous brothers and sold into slavery, becomes a victim of what today we would call "human trafficking." Like many immigrants, Joseph becomes successful through a combination of hard work, good luck, and more than a pinch of heaven's favor. Eventually, after working his way up from slavery to a position of chief advisor to the Egyptian pharaoh, Joseph finds reconciliation with his brothers through his success as an immigrant. This enables him to sponsor his extended family's immigration to Egypt, where they prosper and become numerous.

As is the case with many prosperous and populous immigrant minorities, the Hebrews living in Egypt eventually become victims of the majority population's fear and paranoia. With an appeal to "homeland security," the Egyptians enslave the descendants of Abraham:

> Now a new king arose over Egypt, who did not know Joseph. He said to his people, "Look, the Israelite people are more numerous and more powerful than we. Come, let us deal shrewdly with them, or they will increase and, in the event of war, join our enemies and fight against us and escape from the land." Therefore they set taskmasters over them to oppress them with forced labor. They built supply cities, Pithom and Rameses, for Pharaoh. But the more they were oppressed, the more they multiplied and spread, so that the Egyptians came to dread the Israelites. The Egyptians became ruthless in imposing tasks on the Israelites, and made their lives bitter with hard service in mortar and brick and in every kind of field labor. They were ruthless in all the tasks that they imposed on them. (Exod. 1:8–14)

Responding to the suffering of the Hebrew people, God once again calls them to make a pilgrimage of immigration, this time led by Moses though the waters of the sea, across the Sinai desert and back to Canaan, where a promised land awaits them. It was a long journey ending with the conquest of the land's native populations.

Eventually, as the immigrant Hebrews displace the local Canaanite populations, they cease, for a time, to be a migrant people. As they became more settled, their commitment to righteousness wanes. As they establish a monarchy and an economic power base, the descendants of Abraham become increasingly like the Canaanites among whom they live and from whom they are meant to keep distinct. They become divided, idolatrous, and unfaithful.

Eventually God sends the Hebrews back into exile, back on the immigrant pilgrimage. In the eighth century BCE, the Assyrian Empire swallows up the ten tribes of the Northern Israelite kingdom; more than a century later the Babylonian Empire conquers Jerusalem and the Hebrew territories in the south of Israel. After the fall of Jerusalem, the Babylonian conquerors force tens of thousands of Jews into exile in Babylon; among those exiled are the editors and authors who collect, edit, and record many of the immigrant narratives found in the Bible today.

Part of the biblical witness is the promise to the Hebrews living in Babylonian exile that they will not be an immigrant people forever, but that they will return to their homeland after a period of sojourn. This promise, however, came with an admonition that the pilgrim path of immigrant spirituality not be forgotten. To make sure that the memory of immigration did not fade from the consciousness of the Jewish people, non-Jewish immigrants were to be given special protection when the descendants of Abraham returned to Jerusalem:

> When an alien resides with you in your land, you shall not oppress the alien. The alien who resides with you shall be to you as the citizen among you; you shall love the alien as yourself, for you were aliens in the land of Egypt: I am the LORD your God. (Lev. 19:33–34)

This appeal to memory when dealing with immigrants makes strong use of a "Golden Rule" ethic, that is, one should loves one's neighbor as one loves one's self. It is a bit of religious ethics that was important to Jesus in the New Testament, the part of the Christian Bible to which we turn next.

Immigration in the New Testament

Although the books of the Christian New Testament are not primarily concerned with the immigration of a particular people, the immigration spirituality of the Jewish Bible continues into the Christian Scriptures. This immigrant spirituality is reflected, for example, in the Christmas story as recorded in Matthew's Gospel. In Matthew's version, Jesus' first visitors are foreign Magi who cross political borders to adore the Christ child and to offer him gifts. In the following chapter of Matthew, Jesus and his parents spend time as refugees in Egypt, having been driven out of their homeland for fear of King Herod's violence. In many ways, this story demonstrates divine solidarity with the Gospel of Matthew's first Christian readers, who, like all Jews, suffered displacement in the aftermath of the Roman destruction of Jerusalem.

In Luke's version of the Christmas story, Jesus' family are portrayed as migrants, traveling from Nazareth to Bethlehem while Mary is "great with child." When Jesus is born, wrapped in swaddling clothes, and laid in a manger, he is worshiped first by shepherds who probably were nomads, and may or may not have been Jewish. As in Matthew's Gospel, Luke's telling of the Christmas story places the birth of Christ in the context of migration.

Like the rabbis of Jamnia, the Jewish authors of the four Christian Gospels almost certainly recorded their memories of Jesus' life after—and in response to—the Roman destruction of Jerusalem, the geographic center of their religious tradition. Just as the Babylonian invaders had destroyed the temple for the Jews of the Old Testament, the Romans razed the reconstructed Second Temple for the people of the New Testament. This destruction of the Jerusalem temple is addressed directly in Matthew, Mark, and Luke, the so-called Synoptic (meaning similar) Gospels, as part of the early church's embrace of the Jewish gift of immigrant spirituality.

> As [Jesus] came out of the temple, one of his disciples said to him, "Look, Teacher, what large stones and what large buildings!" Then Jesus asked him, "Do you see these great buildings? Not one stone will be left here upon another; all will be thrown down." (Mark 13:1–2)[4]

While John's Gospel omits Jesus' direct reference to the temple's destruction, it does include Jesus' words to the Samaritan woman at the well, making reference to faith that is removed from the temple's moorings and must exist in exile.

> The woman said to him, "Sir, I see that you are a prophet. Our ancestors worshiped on this mountain, but you say that the place where people must worship is in Jerusalem." Jesus said to her, "Woman, believe me, the hour is coming when you will worship the Father neither on this mountain nor in Jerusalem. You worship what you do not know; we worship what we know, for salvation is from the Jews. But the hour is coming, and is now here, when the true worshipers will worship the Father in spirit and truth, for the Father seeks such as these to worship him. God is spirit, and those who worship him must worship in spirit and truth." (John 4:19–24)

It is no accident that Jesus spoke these words to a Samaritan woman. As a woman and as a Samaritan she was foreign to Jesus, but Jesus looked past the historical walls that separated men from women and Jews from Samaritans and related to her as a neighbor.

The passages about the temple reflect an early Christian community struggling not just with an exile from the physical Jewish temple but also with a spiritual migration out of the Jewish tradition and into the newly formed Christian faith. Just as the rabbis of Jamnia forged the possibility of Jewish faithfulness without a temple, so early Christian leaders developed a system of faithfulness without connection to Jerusalem and without formal ties to traditional Judaism. For Christians, Biblical language that tied the presence of God to the temple in Jerusalem and to the promise of a homeland for God's children became metaphorical.

The Gospels aren't the only part of the New Testament to take up immigration. The most prolific of the Christian New Testament's authors, Paul, was an immigrant. Born in the city of Tarsus, in modern Turkey, Paul was a child of the Jewish diaspora, raised in an immigrant community. While the exact details of Paul's early life are not known, it seems that as a young man he emigrated from Turkey to his ancestral homeland, where his story intersects with and, in many ways, begins to form the story of the Christian church. Paul, then known as Saul of Tarsus, began his relationship with Christianity as a persecutor of the growing Christian Jewish sect. After his conversion he became a missionary—an immigrant evangelist—who traveled around the Mediterranean world establishing churches, first among immigrant Jewish communities and, later, as Paul's travels took him into Gentile communities in Europe, among non-Jews.

Though he lived and died before the destruction of the Jewish temple in Jerusalem, Paul's letters are the earliest surviving Christian writings that imagine a Christian faith capable of migrating away from its connection to Judaism and the Jerusalem temple. Writing to a Gentile audience in the Greek city of Corinth, Paul speaks of the temple in metaphorical terms:

> Do you not know that your body is a temple of the Holy Spirit within you, which you have from God, and that you are not your own? (1 Cor. 6:19)

Like most American Protestants, I grew up believing that Paul's use of the temple metaphor for the human body was meant to keep me from chewing tobacco or smoking dope, and indeed the verse *is* part of a larger warning against carnal vices. But Paul's suggestion that the temple—the terrestrial home of God—was located in the physical bodies of individual believers, rather than in Jerusalem, was a monumental shift. Severed from its connection to a particular place, Christianity became an itinerant faith capable of migration throughout the Roman world and beyond. Indeed, Paul's contention was that Christians were called to an immigrant spiritual life in that believers, though they are residents of earthly realms, are citizens of a heavenly kingdom and must live lives that reflect and commend that citizenship:

> In Christ God was reconciling the world to himself, not counting their trespasses against them, and entrusting the message of reconciliation to us. So we are ambassadors for Christ, since God is making his appeal through us. (2 Cor. 5:19–20a)

It is a theme shared by the apostle Peter:

> Beloved, I urge you as aliens and exiles to abstain from the desires of the flesh that wage war against the soul. Conduct yourselves honorably among the Gentiles, so that, though they malign you as evildoers, they may see your honorable deeds and glorify God when he comes to judge. (1 Pet. 2:11–12)

As the Christian biblical story draws to a close, the apostle and evangelist John records his vision for the end of days, when God's redemption of creation is complete and the divine design for the universe is realized. In John's apocalyptic vision, everyone is an immigrant, as people from every nation take up residence in the City of God, a place made beautiful by human diversity:

> Then I saw a new heaven and a new earth; for the first heaven and the first earth had passed away, and the sea was no more. And I saw the holy city, the new Jerusalem, coming down out of heaven from God, prepared as a bride adorned for her husband. . . . I saw no temple in the city, for its temple is the Lord God the Almighty and the Lamb. And the city has no need of sun or moon to shine on it, for the glory of God is its light, and its lamp is the Lamb. The nations will walk by its light, and the kings of the earth will bring their glory into it. Its gates will never be shut by day—and there will be no night there. People will bring into it the glory and the honor of the nations. (Rev. 21:1–2, 22–26)

The Bible's final vision for a restored heaven and earth is one in which the walls of the City of God have doors that never shut. The kingdom of God has an open border policy, which seems to be consistent with the rest of the Bible's message.

The Bible is not exclusively a book about immigration. There are many interwoven themes that run from Genesis to Revelation, and to ignore any one of these scriptural threads is, for the Christian, to risk living an anemic faith. At this moment in history, though, as immigration issues dominate the American political landscape, Christians living in the United States will do well to reexamine the biblical witness to a God who calls his people to live an immigrant spirituality, to follow the pilgrimage of an immigrant's journey, and to respond with compassion to the needs of those who have made their way to our shores in search of safety from persecution or to take advantage of opportunities to live a better life.

The biblical witness points to a God who walks an immigrant path. Given the testimony of Scripture, it is reasonable to assume that God may send an angel or a saint such as Toribio Romo to accompany and to protect undocumented migrants as they cross the southern border of the United States. It is even more likely to assume that God calls living people of faith to welcome immigrants with compassionate hospitality—as Christians have done throughout their history. That story is the theme of our next chapter.

Chapter 3

Immigration in Church History

Through many dangers, toils and snares
I have already come.
Twas grace that brought me safe thus far
And grace will lead me home.
—John Newton, "Amazing Grace"

During its best historical moments, the Christian church has reflected the immigrant spirituality found in the Bible. The biblical witness has formed the church's identity and has inspired Christians to welcome immigrants, meeting them as neighbors and friends. A complete historical survey of the church's faithfulness (and frequent lack thereof) is beyond the purview of this book, but this chapter takes a look at three periods of church history that are important for American Christians seeking to form a Christian response to the issues that surround migration across the United States' southern border. First, we'll look at the first three hundred years of Christian history, a period of time historians often call the patristic era, when many of the church's foundational beliefs were established. Next, we'll consider the Reformation and the work of Reformed Christians in Geneva who, under the direction of John Calvin, revived the church's commitment to the work of welcoming strangers. Finally, we will go on a brief tour through American history, examining some of the ways that immigrants have shaped the religious landscape of the United States.

The Early Church

According to the New Testament, Jesus' last words were a commission, in which Jesus' earthly followers were instructed to be an emigrant church. In the final verses of Matthew, Jesus says to his gathered disciples,

> "All authority in heaven and on earth has been given to me. Go therefore and make disciples of all nations, baptizing them in the name of the Father and of the Son and of the Holy Spirit, and teaching them to obey everything that I have commanded you. And remember, I am with you always, to the end of the age." (Matt. 28:18–20)

The evangelist Luke, writing in the first chapter of the Acts of the Apostles, records this command in a similar way:

> "You will receive power when the Holy Spirit has come upon you; and you will be my witnesses in Jerusalem, in all Judea and Samaria, and to the ends of the earth." When he had said this, as they were watching, he was lifted up, and a cloud took him out of their sight. (Acts 1:8–9)

This final commandment sparked a religious movement that would transform human history, and the Christian church came to life through the labor of those present for Jesus' last earthly words. Most of those who started the Christian church lived as wayfarers in faithful obedience to Jesus' final command.

The story of Christianity's spread from Jerusalem to Rome via modern-day Turkey and Greece under the leadership of Paul is well known because it is recorded in the New Testament, but Christianity emigrated from the land of Jesus' birth in other directions as well. Both tradition and historical evidence suggest that within a few hundred years of Jesus' death and resurrection, Christianity had spread as far west as Spain and as far north as Great Britain; itinerant evangelists brought the Christian gospel into Africa as far south as Ethiopia and eastward to India.

The missionary migrations of Jesus' earthly followers left an indelible mark on the early church. The Vietnamese-American theologian Peter C. Phan has demonstrated this immigrant self-identification by discovering language of exile and sojourn in the writings of the church fathers, the Christian leaders and thinkers whose writings formed the Christian faith during the church's turbulent first centuries of life. The church fathers often employed the language of immigration to talk about what it meant for Christians to live as a religious minority in the Greco-Roman world.[1]

For example, writing at the end of the first century to the Christians in the Greek city of Corinth, Saint Clement of Rome, who, according to tradition, was the fourth pope, began his epistle with the following words:

> The church of God, living in exile in Rome, to the church of God, exiled in Corinth—to you who are called and sanctified through our Lord Jesus Christ. Abundant grace and peace be yours from God Almighty through Jesus Christ.[2]

Similar words were used by the oddly-named Polycarp, bishop of Smyrna, a city on the Aegean coast of modern-day Turkey, in a letter he wrote to the Christians living in the Macedonian city of Philippi:

> Polycarp and the presbyters with him, to the church of God that sojourns at Philippi; may mercy and peace be multiplied to you from God Almighty and Jesus Christ, our Savior.[3]

Early Christians like Polycarp encouraged their followers to consider themselves as resident aliens in the lands where they resided, sojourners and immigrants who were joined in faith. One of the finest expressions of early Christianity's connection to immigrant spirituality is found in "Letter to Diognetus," an anonymous epistle that probably dates to the end of the second or beginning of the third century of the common era:[4]

> They live in their own countries but only as aliens. They have a share in everything as citizens, and endure everything as foreigners. Every foreign land is their fatherland and yet for them every fatherland is a foreign land . . . They busy themselves on earth, but their citizenship is in heaven.[5]

While immigrant spirituality never disappeared from the life and language of the Christian faith, it's likely that the Christian sense of being foreigners has something to do with the fact that Christianity was largely illegal for the first three hundred years after the life of Christ. As Christianity became legal and, shortly thereafter, was established as the official faith of the Roman Empire, Christians tended less frequently to refer to themselves as exiles and sojourners. Christians eventually rediscovered an immigrant spirituality, but only after certain forms of Christianity became illegal during the Protestant Reformation.

Calvin's Geneva

Geneva's old city is perched on the top of a hill overlooking the place where the Rhone River flows out of Lake Geneva and begins its southward journey to Provence. Today this neighborhood of narrow cobblestone streets is home to upscale restaurants, high-end art dealers, and to Geneva's municipal government. While Switzerland's second-largest city is hardly a tourist mecca on the scale of Paris or Rome, it is a vibrant international community and a place of pilgrimage for serious John Calvin nerds—the devout and the curious. They find their way to *La Cathédrale St-Pierre*, to gaze at the pulpit from whence the father of the Reformed tradition preached sermons that altered the course of Western history, or to imagine the great reformer's derriere nestled into a simple wooden chair, labeled "*Chaise du Cauvin*" and parked like an ecclesiastical non sequitur below the pulpit stairs.

Around the corner from the cathedral, in the heart of Geneva's medieval district, is *La Place du Bourg-de-Four,* an open space that once was Geneva's market. A Genevese gathering place for more than two thousand years, today *La Place du Bourg-de-Four* is a pleasant place to shop for used books or to drink a bottle of Calvinus beer[6] with friends. It also stands as a monument to the ways in which John Calvin helped to revive the practice of immigrant spirituality within the Protestant Reformation.

During the sixteenth century, as religious wars raged throughout Europe, Geneva was a popular destination for Protestant refugees who were drawn to the city for its central location, its relative religious tolerance,[7] and the generous dedication with which the Genevese cared for the poor and welcomed strangers.

What began as a rising tide of immigration in the 1530s and 1540s became a tsunami as Protestant refugees flooded the gates of Geneva. It is estimated that Geneva's population grew from 13,100 in 1550 to 21,400 a decade later,[8] as newcomers from around Europe moved into what already was a crowded city, confined by walls with nowhere to grow but up. So the Genevese built up. To accommodate the influx of religious refugees it became necessary for the owners of buildings within the walled city—under orders from the city fathers—to add an extra story to be used as apartments for the newcomers.[9] Many of these expanded buildings remain today and are especially visible around *La Place du Bourg-de-Four*, where nearly all of the buildings are architecturally different on the top floor—an enduring testimony to the welcoming hospitality extended to Protestant exiles.

As home to international, nongovernmental organizations such as the Red Cross, the International Labor Organization, and the World Health Organization, modern Geneva is a city whose primary industry is the furtherance of world peace.[10] To a casual—if somewhat sentimental—observer drinking Calvinus beer on *La Place du Bourg-de-Four*, it might seem natural that the kindhearted Genevese should build new attics to welcome persecuted religious minorities from around Europe. After all, Geneva is a city with a religiously faithful past and a peaceable present. However, the story of the refugees who moved to Geneva is more complex and fraught with conflict than may be suggested by the quaint beauty of Geneva's old city nearly five hundred years after the fact.

To understand the story of Geneva's refugees and the role religion played in welcoming them, we must begin with the story of Geneva's most famous religious refugee, John Calvin (1509–1564). He joined the Reformation while he was a university student in France, either at the University of Paris where he earned degrees in theology and humanities, or at the University of Orléans, where he studied law.

The exact date of Calvin's conversion is not known, but what remains clear is that by 1535 he was active enough in the furtherance of Reformation ideology that he felt compelled to flee France for the safety of Protestant Basel, in Switzerland. While in Basel he wrote the first edition of the *Institutes of the Christian Religion*, a short book meant to be a primer in basic Reformed thought. (The *Institutes* would expand in subsequent editions; it was to become

Calvin's most important and enduring work.) The *Institutes* was well received, and after a brief—and ill-advised—return to France to settle his financial affairs, Calvin went once more into exile. His intention was to join the Protestant community of Strasbourg, but he chose a circuitous route that took him through Geneva, a city that had accepted the Reformation under the influence and leadership of the preacher William Farel.

Intending to stay a single night in Geneva, Calvin made the mistake of making his presence known to William Farel, who was an intelligent theologian and inspired preacher but was less astute as an organizer of people. Farel was aware of his weakness and in John Calvin he recognized great potential for organized leadership. Farel convinced a reluctant Calvin to stay in Geneva to help organize the newly reformed churches, and with the exception of a brief exile to Strasbourg, John Calvin spent the rest of his life in Geneva, working tirelessly—some might say obsessively—in his capacity as leader of the Genevan Church, striving to create a good, just, and righteous society in the city on a hill.

That righteousness extended to opening Geneva to immigrants and refugees fleeing religious persecution from the parts of Europe that remained Catholic. Many of these refugees felt compelled to leave their homes because Calvin's writing resonated with their spiritual inclinations. In pursuit of his desire to establish a fully Christian civilization in Geneva, Calvin urged the Genevan city fathers to welcome religious exiles not just out of human kindness, but as a matter of religious duty. Writing the city council, he urged them to make Geneva "a firm sanctuary for God amid these horrible commotions and a faithful asylum for the members of Christ."[11]

As mentioned above, the result of Calvin's support for religious refugees is that Geneva's population grew by nearly sixty percent in ten years. This influx of foreigners caused significant distress among many of Geneva's established families, who feared that the foreigners would burden Geneva's economy and change Genevan society with their impassioned piety and their foreign cultural values. Refugees from such places as England, Scotland, the Netherlands, Poland, Hungary, Italy, and Spain brought strange languages with them, while newcomers from France spoke Geneva's native tongue with what, to the Genevese, were foreign accents. Furthermore, Calvin's opponents feared that foreigners living in Geneva might remain committed to their homelands and could not be trusted to act in the best interest of their adopted city.

In 1553 a Geneva city council, hostile to Calvin's vision of Geneva as a "firm sanctuary for God" and "faithful asylum" for religious refugees, passed a series of laws restricting immigration and limiting the rights of immigrants. It became a criminal offense, for example, to host foreigners in Geneva, and foreigners were not allowed to bear arms of any kind. Many of Geneva's citizens, taking a cue from their leaders, subjected Geneva's religious refugees to insults and public mockery. In reference to this period, Calvin wrote, "It is impossible to detail the inhumanity, the barbarism, the savage cruelty with which the enemies of the gospel treated the exiles of Christ whom they had received as co-religionists. And at the same time, the calmness, the moderation, the patience, with which the exiles showed under the indignity are born witness to even by those who inflicted them."[12]

By 1560, Calvin managed politically to outmaneuver his anti-immigrant opponents, and during the final five years of Calvin's life his influence over civic life in Geneva was largely unchallenged.[13] Calvin's commitment to the welcome of religious refugees remained unabated. He even bequeathed a portion of his estate to the "fund for foreigners in need."[14]

The experience of religious refugees in Geneva is instructive for modern Americans who seek to be informed by faith as they form opinions about contemporary immigration issues, because those who sought to limit Geneva's welcome of religious exiles used many of the same arguments employed by those who seek to close America's borders today. In both cases, opposition to immigration was (and is) inspired by a fear that those who are newly-arrived might alter cultural and linguistic norms. In both cases these foreigners were (and are) distrusted, often suspected of harboring secret allegiances to the land of their birth. In both cases the new residents were (and are) blamed for a struggling economy and rising crime rates. In both cases Christians were (and are) pressured by secular voices to stand for "law and order," to preserve tradition, to place the perceived needs of a nation above the real needs of individual immigrants.

In Geneva, the church—under the leadership of John Calvin—remembered the biblical mandate to care for and to welcome strangers, and they put that spiritual principle ahead of concern for what everyone assumed was the well being of the city. In fact, some of the fears of those who wanted to limit immigration to Geneva were realized. The newcomers *did* change the nature of Geneva, but the change wasn't bad. While it is true that Geneva's newer inhabitants favored the strict and often oppressive religiosity of John Calvin, the refugees also helped Geneva to become more cosmopolitan, more educated, and more prosperous—a phenomenon replicated in North America, the subject to which we turn next.

Immigrants and the American Church

After the Reformation, Protestant Christianity quickly became a migrant spiritual movement, or, more accurately, a group of migrant spiritual movements. Much of the Protestant dislocation happened within Europe, as we saw in the foregoing discussion of Geneva's welcome of Calvinist refugees from around Europe. But the Protestant Reformation occurred in an age when, for the first time, European refugees had the option of crossing an ocean in order to put distance between the oppressions of established European churches and the new ways of Protestant piety.

In the two centuries following the Reformation's birth in Germany, waves of Protestant immigrants made their way across the Atlantic to settle in North America from every part of Europe. Lutherans came from Germany and Scandinavia; Anabaptists from Switzerland, the Netherlands, Ukraine, and Canada; Baptists, Quakers, and Anglicans from England; and Calvinists from Scotland, England, the Netherlands, and France. It was a religious melting pot unlike any the world had seen up to that time.

For many Protestant immigrants to North America, faith brought meaning to the experience of migration, and for American Christians struggling to make sense of contemporary immigration policy as people of faith, perhaps no spiritual understanding of a physical journey is more important than that of a group of English Calvinists who crossed the Atlantic on the *Mayflower* in 1620 and settled in New England. They were directionally challenged (their intention was to reach Virginia) and ill-prepared (they had few provisions, had no idea how to farm or fish, and were, therefore, largely dependant upon the kindness of local native people for survival)[15] wanderers who saw their migration as divinely inspired.

The Calvinists on the *Mayflower* believed the voyage that had taken them from the comfort of England to the wilds of North America at great cost in treasure and in human life was a journey whose purpose was to glorify God and to advance the Christian faith. They were not the last to hold their immigration in such high spiritual esteem.

Indeed, subsequent generations of Americans have shared the Pilgrims' view that theirs was a journey of spiritual importance. Such a spiritual interpretation of their journey is evident in the name by which Americans call the band of travelers who crossed the Atlantic Ocean on the *Mayflower*. The word "pilgrim," which can be defined as "one who travels to a shrine or holy place,"[16] was rarely used by Pilgrims to describe themselves (they called themselves "saints").[17] But in the popular American imagination, the *Mayflower's* cargo of Calvinists has been called Pilgrims to affirm not only that these early European settlers were faithful Christians, but also that North America was, and is, a holy place.

So strong is the American drive to remember the *Mayflower*'s passengers as religious Pilgrims that a broad cultural amnesia has arisen around the fact that many of those who traveled on the *Mayflower* seemed to have had no religious motivation for the trip. After having assigned to the whole group the religious motivation of a minority, we have also remembered them as members of the wrong Christian denomination. Though they are remembered as Puritans, they were, in fact, nonconforming Separatists, the Puritans being reform-minded Anglicans who wanted the Church of England officially to adopt Calvinism and the Pilgrims being more rigid Calvinists who wanted to start independent, self-governing congregations. (They soon joined together in the New World, which adds to our historical confusion of the two groups.)

Regardless of what we now call the English Calvinists who crossed the Atlantic on the *Mayflower*, theirs was a religious migration that informs Americans' spiritual self-identity to this day. If, in our modern corporate imagination, we are willing to remember the Puritans/Pilgrims (many of whom were neither), as immigrants whose journey fulfilled a divine purpose, might we also be willing to assign such holy motives to modern immigrants who enter the United States from the south, often without papers? Is there really any qualitative difference between an English Calvinist living in the seventeenth century and a Catholic or evangelical Mexican or Guatemalan immigrant today?

Many modern immigrants from Mexico and other Latin American countries believe they also are pilgrims who understand their journeys to be inspired by God for the purpose of bringing renewal and revival to American churches. In his book *Christians at the Border*, the Guatemalan-American biblical scholar M. Daniel Carroll R. notes the sense of divine purpose shared by many evangelical immigrants from Latin America and asks,

> [C]ould what we are witnessing in this country be part of a divinely directed global phenomenon? Is God bringing millions of Hispanics to the United States to revitalize the Christian churches here and to present to those who do not yet believe the opportunity to turn to Christ in their search for a new life? Many Hispanics and pastors sincerely believe that God has led them here for a purpose: to play an important role in the revival of the Christian faith in this country.[18]

Professor Carroll isn't the first or the only religious leader to suggest that immigration provides a spiritual benefit for the people living and worshiping in the receiving country. For the late Pope John Paul II, immigrants are a "sacramental presence":

> Solidarity means taking responsibility for those in trouble. For Christians, the migrant is not merely an individual to be respected in accordance with the norms established by law, but a person whose presence challenges them and whose needs become an obligation for their responsibility. "What have you done to your brother?" (Cf. Gen 4:9). The answer should not be limited to what is imposed by law, but should be made in the manner of solidarity.
>
> [Humans], particularly if [they are] weak, defenseless, driven to the margins of society, [are] a sacrament of Christ's presence (cf. Mt 25:40, 45).
>
> . . . It is the Church's task not only to present constantly the Lord's teaching of faith, but also to indicate its appropriate application to the various situations which the changing times continue

> to create. Today the illegal migrant comes before us like that "stranger" in whom Jesus asks to be recognized. To welcome him and to show him solidarity is a duty of hospitality and fidelity to Christian identity itself.[19]

It is worth asking if the concept of immigration as a journey of spiritual purpose died with the English Pilgrims. Might immigration from Latin America be a phenomenon that's also divinely inspired? Certainly immigrant churches are thriving. Maybe John Paul II was correct to say that Christ's sacramental presence is with the immigrant. Maybe M. Daniel Carroll R. is right when he points to the evangelizing potential of immigrants. We can't know that for sure, but the Christian history we've uncovered in this chapter certainly suggests that they're in a well-established tradition of caring for the immigrant not just out of kindness, or because such welcome is rooted in the Christian tradition, but because God speaks in fresh ways through the mouths of immigrants.

For most American Christians, embracing immigrants as bearers of the sacramental presence of Christ, as fellow believers on a pilgrim path, would be a return to our religion's spiritual roots. Doing so would acknowledge that the migrant spirituality found in Scripture and in the earliest Christian churches, a spirituality that was revived in European Protestantism and in the Protestantism of many early European settlers in North America, is still alive. This would be a natural affirmation for those who believe human nature seldom changes and that God is the same yesterday, today, and tomorrow.

Other Immigrant Stories

Having suggested that the experience of immigration has helped to form the faith and spirituality of European Protestant immigrants to North America, it is important to remember that not all immigrants to North America were European Protestants, yet the spiritual impact of immigration remains a constant theme in a variety of immigrant communities.

For early American immigrants from Africa, the journey across the Atlantic was not voluntary. Kidnapped, sold, enslaved, and transported in unimaginable and often fatal squalor, the African immigrants to North America incorporated the experience of their forced migration into the practice of Christianity, a religion they adopted and adapted from those who kept them enslaved.

It is safe to say that the themes of exile and of foreign sojourn are so important in African American spirituality that it is impossible to treat them with anything approaching justice in a book that isn't expressly about those themes. Looking for a concise way to talk about immigrant spirituality in the African American context, I met up with Jim Bennett, a professor of American religious history at Santa Clara University. Jim specializes in the history of African American Christianity, and after we'd eaten a couple of burritos at a *taqueria* near my home in San José, I asked him for a succinct way to talk about how the experience of forced immigration affected African American spirituality.

"The story of the exodus becomes central," he told me. "Sometimes Moses is almost as important as Jesus, and whereas for the Pilgrims and other white Christians America was like the promised land, for African Americans it was Egypt.

"But it's not as if the desire was to return to Africa. There always has been a sense that since African Americans built America they would stay here. The focus has always been upon making America the promised land."

As Jim points out, there exists an important difference between European-American Protestants' views of immigration and African American Protestants'. One tradition sees immigration as an act of faithfulness and the other remembers immigration as one of the great crimes in human history, an exile to be escaped in favor of a promised land.

Most of the descendants of African slaves living in the United States are Protestants, but Protestantism is not the only variant of Christianity that has influenced the spiritual landscape of North America through immigration. Roman Catholic Christians have been migrating to North America since the earliest years of active European settlement, but the largest waves of Catholic immigration into the United States began in the middle of the nineteenth century when millions of Irish crossed the Atlantic to escape the Potato Famine. After the Irish came Catholic Germans and French Canadians, and, by the end of World War I, millions of Catholics had come from southern and eastern Europe—Italians mostly, but also Slovaks, Slovenians, Poles, Hungarians, Ukrainians, and Lithuanians.[20] More recent waves of Catholic immigration have come from Latin America, the Philippines, and Viet Nam, and each wave of immigration has left its mark on American Catholicism, molding it to reflect the immigrant spirituality of those who call the Catholic Church their spiritual home. As we consider the spiritual nature of immigration, Roman Catholicism is, perhaps, the most important Christian community to watch, as Roman Catholics from Latin America constitute the largest religious demographic among immigrants at the beginning of the third millennium's second decade.

In all of its manifestations, American Christianity is an immigrant faith, born of immigrants and formed by the stories of immigration. That some American Christians do not feel compelled to support those who continue to immigrate to the United States calls to mind a particularly well-articulated observation made by Bill Bryson in his book *Made in America*.

> If one attitude can be said to characterize America's regard for immigration over the past two hundred years it is the belief that while immigration was unquestionably a wise and prescient thing in the case of one's parents or grandparents, it really ought to stop now. For two hundred years succeeding generations of Americans have persuaded themselves that the country faced imminent social dislocation, and eventual ruin, at the hands of the grasping foreign hordes pouring through her ports.[21]

Bryson's comment is, I suppose, an ironic re-articulation of a very biblical concept:

> When an alien resides with you in your land, you shall not oppress the alien. The alien who resides with you shall be to you as the citizen among you; you shall love the alien as yourself, for you were aliens in the land of Egypt: I am the LORD your God. (Lev. 19:33–34)

For me—as for many American descendents of European immigrants, honoring this biblical concept requires remembering the conditions under which my ancestors immigrated. Often such memories can be found in literature. For example, in his classic children's story *Kidnapped,* Robert Louis Stevenson describes an encounter with a boat of Scottish Highland emigrants as it prepares to set sail for America:

> In the mouth of Loch Aline we found a great sea-going ship at anchor; and this I supposed at first to be one of the King's cruisers which were kept along that coast, both summer and winter, to prevent communication with the French. As we got a little nearer, it became plain she was a ship of merchandise; and what still more puzzled me, not only her decks, but the sea-beach also, were quite black with people, and skiffs were continually plying to and fro between them. Yet nearer, and there began to come to our ears a great sound of mourning, the people on board and those on the shore crying and lamenting one to another so as to pierce the heart.
>
> Then I understood this was an emigrant ship bound for the American colonies.
>
> We put the ferry-boat alongside, and the exiles leaned over the bulwarks, weeping and reaching out their hands to my fellow-passengers, among whom they counted some near friends. How long this might have gone on I do not know, for they seemed to have no sense of time: but at last the captain of the ship, who seemed near beside himself (and no great wonder) in the midst of this crying and confusion, came to the side and begged us to depart.
>
> Thereupon Neil sheered off; and the chief singer in our boat struck into a melancholy air, which was presently taken up both by the emigrants and their friends upon the beach, so that it sounded from all sides like a lament for the dying. I saw the tears run down the cheeks of the men and women in the boat, even as they bent at the oars; and the circumstances and the music of the song (which is one called "Lochaber no more") were highly affecting even to myself.[22]

As a Presbyterian with more than a few drops of Scottish blood in my veins, it's easy for me to be moved by Stevenson's description of those forced to move by the brutal English clearing of the Highlands. Many of the people who founded American Presbyterianism immigrated in similar conditions. Their stories formed who I am, just as all Americans who are not American Indians have been formed by the story of immigration.

If, as a Presbyterian and as the descendant of Scottish immigrants, I am able to recognize human suffering and the necessity of immigration in an account of Scottish immigration in the middle of the eighteenth century, but cannot recognize human suffering or affirm the necessity of immigration when I hear the stories of those who escape political oppression or economic depravity in Mexico and Central America, then my Christian faith has failed me. I have not learned from my history. I have not remembered my own story.

If we learn anything from the Christian church's relationship to immigration it is that it is hardly a radical theological innovation to suggest that Christians should extend a warm and neighborly welcome to immigrants, even if those immigrants don't have proper documentation. It is a fact, however, that many objections to the welcome of immigrants are not related to church history. We'll consider further objections in the next chapter.

Chapter 4

On Rendering to Caesar and God

The worst casualty to truth comes after it has been so manipulated that the manipulators can redefine it to suit their own ends. This represents the ultimate attempt of Caesar to usurp the role of God.

—*Robert McAfee Brown*[1]

A reasonable objection often is raised to the suggestions that the Bible and Christian tradition direct persons of faith to extend hospitality toward immigrants who may reside illegally in a host country: illegal immigration is illegal. Regardless of any pro-immigrant sentiments that may be expressed in Scripture, there also is a biblical mandate to honor and obey the laws of God-ordained governments. In his letter to the Christians living in Rome, Paul admonishes his followers:

> Let every person be subject to the governing authorities; for there is no authority except from God, and those authorities that exist have been instituted by God. Therefore whoever resists authority resists what God has appointed, and those who resist will incur judgment. For rulers are not a terror to good conduct, but to bad. Do you wish to have no fear of the authority? Then do what is good, and you will receive its approval; for it is God's servant for your good. But if you do what is wrong, you should be afraid, for the authority does not bear the sword in vain! It is the servant of God to execute wrath on the wrongdoer. Therefore one must be subject, not only because of wrath but also because of conscience. (Rom. 13:1–5)

Later in the New Testament, Peter sounds a similar theme.

> For the Lord's sake accept the authority of every human institution, whether of the emperor as supreme, or of governors, as sent by him to punish those who do wrong and to praise those who do right. For it is God's will that by doing right you should silence the ignorance of the foolish. As servants of God, live as free people, yet do not use your freedom as a pretext for evil. Honor everyone. Love the family of believers. Fear God. Honor the emperor. (1 Pet. 2:13–17)

There is an eloquent simplicity to this argument. The law is the law, and Christians are not called to be criminals. Moreover, in the United States, Christians have a strong commitment to the separation of church and state, which often is understood to mean that faith is a private matter, applicable to personal matters but having little effect on life outside the home and the church.

It is doubtful, however, that either Paul or Peter would have advocated following human laws without a thoughtful and prayerful moral analysis of those laws. For example, it's hard to imagine either author subscribing to the idea that Christians should obey the laws that made Christianity illegal in the Roman Empire. According to church tradition, both apostles were martyred without recanting their Christianity, their deaths mandated by the laws of the state of that time. Both apostles, and many of their fellow martyrs, understood that faithful Christians are responsible to disobey those human laws that run contrary to biblical values. Christians are to be spiritual immigrants, citizens of a kingdom not of this world. A Christian's proper loyalty is directed first to the kingdom of God before it is pledged to an earthly nation, and that hierarchy of fidelity necessarily causes us to question laws even when set down by an emperor whose reign was established by God.

Immigrants as Refugees

The need for such questioning did not end in the early years of the Christian faith. I first faced the need to question the laws of the American government in 1985. During my senior year in high school my

Spanish teacher, who also was a member of my church, recruited me to help translate for a family of El Salvadoran refugees who were receiving sanctuary from an interfaith group of activists in my home town.

In the 1980s, El Salvador was a mess. A civil war in this tiny Central American nation had become a proxy conflict for the opposing forces of the Cold War, and by the time the family for whom we provided sanctuary came to us, the United States government was pouring out more than a million dollars a day to pay for the El Salvadoran army's fight against communist rebels.

Historians will debate and form varying opinions about the justice and efficacy of the fight against communism in El Salvador, but regardless of what one may think of the war, any but the most Machiavellian of capitalism's true believers would condemn as immoral and ruthless the methods of warfare used by the U.S.-backed Salvadoran army. U.S.-funded-and-trained death squads carried out extrajudicial executions and "disappearances" with terrifying regularity. Torture was commonplace. The El Salvadoran military targeted civilian populations as a matter of course.

From the danger and tragedy that was life in El Salvador in the mid-eighties, Efraín Baños and his two teenaged sons, René and Edwin, moved to California's North Coast and into the care of the Mendocino Sanctuary Coalition.

There was nothing legal about the presence of the Baños family in Northern California. Efraín was a wanted man in El Salvador, a criminal on the run from the law. Before leaving the family home in the El Salvadoran capital, San Salvador, Efraín had worked as a chauffeur for Archbishop Oscar Romero and, after the Archbishop's assassination, as an ambulance driver. His "crime" was showing up with his ambulance at the site of a military attack on a civilian neighborhood in San Salvador and saving the lives of some of the army's intended targets.

Despite warnings from the military, Efraín continued to drive his ambulance. In retaliation, the military death squads murdered his wife and abducted his two boys, forcing them into a military academy to be used as cannon fodder in the civil war. Finally, Efraín left his ambulance, found and rescued his sons, and headed north with his kids. They traveled as illegal migrants through Guatemala, Mexico, and into the United States, where they remained as illegal residents of my community until obtaining the falsified documents Efraín needed to apply for amnesty under the Immigration Reform and Control Act of 1986.

It is hard to imagine a morally viable reason for American Christians not to have come to the aid of the Baños family, even if such aid was given in contradiction to the laws of the United States. Had Efraín kept his family in El Salvador, his sons would have been forced to fight as child soldiers, and it is likely that Efraín himself would have been murdered by the military regime.

However law-abiding and even "patriotic" it may have seemed to turn over Efraín and his boys to the border patrol, to have been complicit in the extradition of the Baños family would have been a murderous act. It would have been indefensible for those guided by a biblical ethic or by any other reasonable set of moral standards.

In the end we didn't save Efraín's life. Many years later my high school Spanish teacher told me that Efraín was murdered in San Salvador, where he had returned after the end of the civil war, but I'm glad we gave him an extra ten years with his sons, and I feel privileged to have played a small part in his American sojourn. My experience acting as a translator for the Baños family was transformative. I translated, on and off, for the duration of my final year in high school and went to college with a healthy skepticism toward the idea that American laws are good simply because they are American laws.

Regardless of the biblical mandate to be subject to "governing authorities," and to "honor the emperor," Christians have a strong tradition of finding it necessary sometimes to resist immoral laws. According to the biblical witness, Christians' responsibility to break unjust laws is both literally and literarily the other side of the coin from the commandment that we obey earthly rulers.

During the final days of his life and ministry some of Jesus' detractors wanted to catch him in a rhetorical trap, forcing him to make a statement that either would anger and alienate his followers or would run him afoul of the Roman empire:

> Then the Pharisees went and plotted to entrap him in what he said. So they sent their disciples to him, along with the Herodians, saying, "Teacher, we know that you are sincere, and teach the way

> of God in accordance with truth, and show deference to no one; for you do not regard people with partiality. Tell us, then, what you think. Is it lawful to pay taxes to the emperor, or not?" But Jesus, aware of their malice, said, "Why are you putting me to the test, you hypocrites? Show me the coin used for the tax." And they brought him a denarius. Then he said to them, "Whose head is this, and whose title?" They answered, "The emperor's." Then he said to them, "Give therefore to the emperor the things that are the emperor's, and to God the things that are God's." When they heard this, they were amazed; and they left him and went away. (Matt. 22:15–22)

The Pharisees were Jewish lay scholars who generally opposed Roman rule, and, therefore, resented paying Roman taxes. The Herodians were allies of Herod, the non-Jewish puppet king of Judea. Herod and the Herodians were supported by taxation. So it was an impossible question. Jesus' interlocutors expected Jesus to offend someone no matter what his answer, but Jesus deflected the question by giving an answer neither side expected: give to the emperor what belongs to the emperor and give to God that which belongs to God. Be a good citizen *and* be a person of abiding faith. Usually, it's both possible and mandatory that we live in obedience both to earthly rulers and to the call that God places in our lives, though sometimes God calls us to break the law when the law is immoral or contradicts the mandates of faith.

The case of Efraín and his sons is such a case, and those of us who broke the law to protect the Baños family did so as part of an important Christian tradition in which Christians have found it necessary to break the law—to render to God what belongs to God, even if it means withholding from Caesar what Caesar claims. We broke the law in the same way (though with much less courage needed) as the earliest Christians broke the law. Many centuries later this same spirit of faithful law-breaking inspired Christians living under Communist regimes to endure torture, gulags, and death as punishment for keeping the faith; during the Reformation, Protestant Christians broke the law in various parts of Europe by choosing not to be Catholic. Christians engaged in illegal activity when they harbored runaway slaves in North America in the nineteenth century, and when they hid Jews from Nazis in Europe during the Second World War.

Christians have a long tradition of breaking the law for the sake of God's kingdom.

Two years after my experience translating for the Baños family, the plight of another refugee from El Salvador challenged me to break American laws in support of the kingdom of God. I was working with Central American refugees in San Francisco at an Episcopalian community center in the city's Mission District. Doing the work, I became friendly with Maria, an elderly woman who had suffered a stroke and was confined to a wheelchair. I spent one afternoon a week caring for her and talking with her. Like Efraín Baños, she had been an associate of Archbishop Oscar Romero, and in those days, any friend of Oscar Romero's was perceived to be an enemy of the state, even if—as was the case of my friend—your only crime was being a teacher committed to improving literacy among the poor.

During the time I lived and worked in San Francisco, Maria had the opportunity to apply for amnesty under the Immigration Reform and Control Act of 1986, the same law through which Efraín and his sons had become legal residents in the United States using falsified papers, and like Efraín and his sons, she didn't qualify to apply for amnesty because she hadn't been living long enough in the United States. Her convalescence notwithstanding, if she had returned to El Salvador, the country's death squads very likely would have killed her because of her association with Romero. So I falsified papers for her so that, like the Baños family, she could qualify for residency. I lied to the U.S. government, saying that I'd known her for enough time that she appeared to qualify for amnesty.

I've never regretted my youthful decision to practice outlaw compassion. I wasn't ready to send my friend back to El Salvador and a probable death. I wasn't prepared to render unto Caesar what belonged to God.

In telling the stories of the El Salvadoran refugees with whom I worked as a young man, it's worth noting that U.S. immigration law generally makes a provision for leniency toward refugees, who are defined as people whose lives would be endangered in their homelands because of their political or religious views. Both Efraín and Maria certainly should have qualified as refugees under American law, and they would have had they been from another country, but because the United States supported the same government that threatened the lives of Maria, Efraín and his children, it did not welcome Salvadorans fleeing the war as refugees.[2] So in some ways, by helping El Salvadoran refugees, I was helping my country to uphold its better traditions, even if such fidelity to tradition had to happen outside of the law.

Immigrants Seeking Economic Opportunity

It must be acknowledged that most of the immigrants who cross the U.S./Mexico border are not fleeing civil war but are motivated to head north in order to escape poverty. Though warfare and political violence continue to be factors in some immigration from Mexico and Central America, the overwhelming majority of those who migrate north are poor, unemployed, and willing to do difficult work for below-market wages. Many Americans find it easer to welcome war refugees than unemployed laborers, so it is reasonable to ask if the immigrant spirituality of a biblical faith calls Christians to provide sanctuary and protection for those who violate American laws by crossing the border in search of employment and economic opportunities that aren't available in Mexico or Central America.

In addressing this question it's helpful to note that the Bible calls believers to exercise economic compassion more often than it calls people of faith to engage in any other moral or ethical behavior, and it's interesting to note that the Bible does not make the explicit suggestion that only aliens who are refugees and victims of war should be welcomed and shown justice. The Bible does, however, make a specific provision for the care of those who immigrate because they are poor and, presumably, are seeking a better life for themselves and their families.

The book of Leviticus, in a list of laws that set the parameters for the establishment of a righteous society, mandates that those who enjoy an abundance of wealth must make provision for the poor, in general, and for impoverished immigrants, in particular.

> When you reap the harvest of your land, you shall not reap to the very edges of your field, or gather the gleanings of your harvest. You shall not strip your vineyard bare, or gather the fallen grapes

> of your vineyard; you shall leave them for the poor and the alien: I am the LORD your God. (Lev. 19:9–10)

The commandment is repeated a few chapters later (Lev. 23:22) and expounded in more detail in Deuteronomy:

> When you reap your harvest in your field and forget a sheaf in the field, you shall not go back to get it; it shall be left for the alien, the orphan, and the widow, so that the LORD your God may bless you in all your undertakings. When you beat your olive trees, do not strip what is left; it shall be for the alien, the orphan, and the widow. When you gather the grapes of your vineyard, do not glean what is left; it shall be for the alien, the orphan, and the widow. Remember that you were a slave in the land of Egypt; therefore I am commanding you to do this. (Deut. 24:19–22)

In the Old Testament, aliens—that is, foreigners residing in Israel on a permanent or semi-permanent basis—were classified, along with widows and orphans, as people to be helped. But even without the biblical mandate to care for poor foreigners sojourning in the land, the rules of common decency and simple compassion should be motivation enough for Christians—and all persons of good conscience—to respond to economically motivated, undocumented migration across the U.S./Mexico border.

Between 1995 and 2003 I sat on the board of Presbyterian Border Ministry, a binational organization that engages in evangelistic, educational, medical, and economic development work along the U.S./Mexico border. As a member of the PBM board I visited the border region twice a year, and during a visit to Juarez, across the border from El Paso, Texas, in the Mexican state of Chihuahua, my wife and I came across a girl looking forlornly down a storm drain. It was an odd enough sight to cause us to stop and ask what she was trying to find down the hole. She pointed to what looked like a credit card that lay just beyond her reach. It was, she told us, the time card she needed to go to work at one of the many *maquiladoras*, or manufacturing plants, that had grown up along the border to take advantage of the free trade rules established by the North America Free Trade Agreement (NAFTA). With tears in her eyes, she informed us that she would lose her job if she could not retrieve the card that she had dropped down the storm drain.

It's likely that the loss of her job would have been a serious economic hardship for the girl's family. After the ratification of NAFTA, *maquiladoras* began employing tens of thousands of early adolescent girls, paying them wages that were higher than they could earn elsewhere in Mexico but less than the minimum wage for adults under Mexican law. As a result, it often was easier for adolescent girls to find work than it was for their parents. Frequently, teenaged daughters were the sole breadwinners in their families. While the laws governing working conditions in *maquiladoras* generally are good, enforcement of those laws usually is lax; often the people employed in *maquiladoras* are abused, exposed to dangerous toxins, and made to work dangerously long hours.

The girl's job was saved that day because she was chewing gum, which I stuck to the end of a long piece of cardboard ripped from a discarded box nearby. The gum was just adhesive enough to lift the time card off the ground and stay attached to the cardboard for the three-foot journey from the bottom of the hole to the steel grate through which the card had dropped.

As happy as I was to have helped provide for the girl's continued employment, when we parted ways I had a heavy heart. It would have been better to provide her with an education, or at least employment outside of a *maquiladora*. Since that day in Juarez I have become the father of two daughters and a foster daughter. Given the choice between asking my daughters to work in a manufacturing plant or making an illegal crossing into the United States, I doubt I would stay in Mexico, and I cannot blame those who leave the desperate poverty of Latin America to travel north in search of a more promising future.

National Borders, and a Short History Lesson

When we speak of making an "illegal" crossing north into the United States, it becomes important to address the issue of the border itself and whether or not restricting human traffic across the border is rendering to Caesar the things that properly are Caesar's, or if the border is merely a construction invented by Caesar at the expense of what belongs to God.

Most Americans do not question the moral validity of the border that separates the United States of America from the United States of Mexico, and some may even believe that the border was—in some way—established by God, perhaps in confirmation of the old American notion of a manifest destiny through which the United States would be established as a single country from sea to shining sea.

Yet to say that the U.S./Mexico border was authored by God or even established according to generally accepted moral standards is to say something remarkable about the Mexican-American War, which established much of the border between the United States and Mexico.

Like all wars, the Mexican-American War has a complicated history that is interpreted differently on either side of the border, but what seems to be without debate is that by the middle of the nineteenth century the United States increasingly saw itself as a nation whose borders should span the North American continent, a belief enshrined as divinely inspired by the doctrine of manifest destiny. Inconveniently, the northern half of Mexico stood in the way of manifest destiny, and in 1845 the administration of James Polk offered to buy the northern half of Mexico (what is now the American Southwest, including all or parts of Texas, New Mexico, Colorado, Wyoming, Utah, Arizona, and California) for twenty-five million dollars. Mexico refused to sell.

In the meantime, Mexico was losing control of its vast, sparsely inhabited northern territories. Slave-owning American settlers in Texas demanded the right to hold slaves in violation of Mexican law; they revolted when Mexico refused their demands. American immigrants in California also started a rebellion, declaring independence from Mexico and a desire to join the United States.

So the United States invaded Mexico. Congress declared war against Mexico on May 13, 1846, and invaded its southern neighbor. By February of 1848, after the United States captured Mexico City, Mexico surrendered and signed the Treaty of Guadalupe Hidalgo, in which Mexico was forced to sell to its northern neighbor all, or parts of, Texas, New Mexico, Arizona, California, Nevada, Utah, Colorado, and Wyoming for eighteen million dollars. Besides losing more than half its territory, Mexico also lost the ports of Galveston, San Diego, Long Beach, and San Francisco (leaving Mexico with Vera Cruz as its only major seaport). Mexico lost all oil in Texas and

California as well as California's gold, Nevada's silver, the mineral wealth of the intermountain west, and unmeasured agrarian, fishing, and timber resources. To say that Mexico was the victim of one of history's great acts of imperialist thievery is to engage in an epic understatement.

Though many Americans at the time supported the war, it was not universally accepted as a moral invasion of a sovereign state. While he was still a congressman from Illinois, Abraham Lincoln questioned the morality of this military campaign of conquest by pointing out that the first American blood shed in the war was spilled on Mexican territory. Years after fighting in the war, Ulysses S. Grant called the Mexican-American War "the most unjust [war] ever waged by a stronger against a weaker nation." Robert E. Lee, who also participated in the Mexican-American War (and who was not famous for agreeing with Ulysses S. Grant) shared this sentiment.[3]

Given this checkered history, it might be argued that immigrants from Mexico who enter territory taken from their homeland in a morally reprehensible war have a legitimate right to sojourn in the American Southwest. Adding to this claim is the fact that most Mexicans are descended—at least in part—from the original inhabitants of North America who were crossing the bit of land we now call a border thousands of years before the first Europeans set foot in the Americas. By contrast, my people (most of them anyway) came from the British Isles and other parts of northern Europe by way of Minnesota, Ohio, and Iowa. It's not a heritage that would seem to give me an inherent right to own property on stolen land in California.

The moral ambiguity that surrounds the establishment of the U.S./ Mexico border is not unique. The world is full of ethically dubious international demarcations. Many—like the U.S./Mexico border—were established through bloody conflict and conquest, others were drawn by colonial powers with little concern for the wishes of common people, and international borders change all the time. To suggest that any nation's borders are the result of divine cartography is to ascribe to God what often is the result of violence and human sinfulness. This seems rather presumptuous.

To say that Christians should respond to the immigration crisis by supporting the enforcement of increasingly strict national anti-immigration laws, even if the enforcement of such laws causes human suffering, is to say that international borders are more deserving of protection than are the humans who cross them. Such an approach renders to Caesar what belongs to God. It does not reflect the Bible's word or spirit. It's hard to imagine Jesus or any of the great saints of the Christian church taking such a view of immigration.

Am I My Immigrant Brother's Keeper?

Those who argue in favor of a more punitive response to undocumented migration across the U.S./Mexico border often appeal to a sense of justice that is rooted in an offended sense of fairness. Is it fair, for example, for American taxpayers to provide public services and the benefits of life in the United States to those who have entered our nation without permission, who reside without legal documentation, and who pay no taxes? Should the children of such immigrants be given a free public education? Should they be allowed to drive on publicly funded roads or be given the protection and conveniences of public services? Is it just or equitable for American citizens to underwrite the good lives of those who enter our nation and stay without visas, while we make immigration difficult for those who desire to come into our country legally? Is the presence of undocumented immigrants not, fundamentally, unfair?

Such questions become particularly acute during times of economic uncertainty, when the cost of providing services to undocumented immigrants can feel like an untenable expense to communities, states, and a federal government strapped for cash. This issue was evident in the ways Americans spoke about health care during the summer of 2009, when Rep. Joe Wilson (R-NC) interrupted President Obama's speech to a joint session of Congress, shouting, "You lie!" when the President claimed that his vision for health care reform did not include free health care for illegal immigrants. Wilson's outburst earned him accolades from those who favor increased enforcement of immigration laws.

These are fair questions that must be addressed, first of all, with truth telling. The truth is that undocumented immigrants are not a financial burden on American society. In fact, while it is true that undocumented immigrants receive the same public benefits and protections that are extended to all residents, many observers of immigration issues argue that the presence of undocumented immigrants provides a net financial benefit to those who reside in the United States legally.

The *New York Times* reported that an estimated three-quarters of undocumented immigrants provide their employers with easily obtained false Social Security numbers, which generate billions of dollars of Social Security withholdings each year, money that will never be collected by the workers and which accounts for ten percent of the annual Social Security surplus.[4] Other monies withheld include state and federal income tax and various state and local taxes and fees. Also, undocumented immigrants spend most of the money they earn doing menial work for minimal pay, rather than saving it or even sending it to relatives. They are working-class consumers who must feed, clothe, and house themselves by patronizing American businesses. The money they spend in this country generates taxable income for merchants, and, in most states, is subject to sales tax.

In addition to the public funds generated by the economic activity of undocumented immigrants, the broader American community derives a financial benefit from the low wages at which most undocumented migrants are willing to work. The food, landscaping, child care, and cleaning services we enjoy all come to us at a discount thanks to the low wages paid to undocumented workers.

What it boils down to is this: If we are to avoid bearing false witness we must tell the truth. Undocumented migrants are not a financial burden for taxpaying American citizens and legal residents; in fact, they contribute economically to this country.

An additional question around the fairness of undocumented immigration arises when those who enter and reside in the United States are contrasted with legal immigrants who spend significant amounts of money, wait long periods of time, and complete reams of paperwork in order to obtain proper documentation. Is it fair for undocumented immigrants to "jump to the head of the line," entering the United States before those who attempt to play by the rules?

This also is a fair question that must be addressed with truth telling. Those who live in the United States illegally have exactly no advantage over legal immigrants. It is entirely worth noting that while I know many immigrants, both legal and undocumented, I've never met a legal immigrant who would trade places with someone who traveled north without proper documentation, nor have I met an undocumented immigrant who would have turned down the opportunity to enter and to reside in the United States with a visa.

The suggestion that it is unfair to offer amnesty or other kinds of favorable treatment to undocumented immigrants is further complicated by the fact that many undocumented immigrants did not choose to come to the United States. A significant portion of those living in the undocumented shadows of American society came to the United States as children. While researching this book I met, for example, a young woman named Anahí, who came to the United States when she was twelve years old. When I met her, she had completed three years in the California State University system and was trying to secure the financial aid necessary to complete her final year. While carrying a full academic load, Anahí worked between forty and sixty hours a week and she provided care for her chronically ill mother. She was articulate and bright, the kind of person for whom the world should provide a host of enticing career paths, but because she was undocumented, her options for future employment are limited by the fact that she cannot legally get a job, and by the fact that the state of California does not issue driver's licenses to undocumented migrants. Even if she found a good job, she would be unable to commute to that job in an automobile.

Anahí's situation is not unique. No one knows for sure how many undocumented children live in the United States, but there could be millions of such children. For most undocumented children, the United States is home. They speak English and have been educated in American schools. Culturally, they are indistinguishable from their friends and classmates who are U.S. citizens. Most undocumented children grow up as Americans. Frequently they get married here and have children. Issues of fairness get murky. Is it fair, for example, to ask an undocumented person who has lived in the United States since childhood to "return" to the land of his or her birth, leaving family and community behind, to apply for a visa that may be denied? It doesn't seem like it.

Yet even if it is unfair for undocumented immigrants, regardless of their stories, to receive amnesty, fairness may not, ultimately, be the defining issue for those desiring to build lives that are guided and molded by the Christian Scriptures. When the Bible calls Christians to live lives that are marked with a concern for justice, it is not suggesting that everything in life should be fair. Justice is not the same as fairness.

As I consider the stories mentioned in this chapter, that of Efraín and his sons, of Maria, of the unnamed *maquiladora* employee from Juarez, and Anahí, the young California college student who came to the United States as a child and who is "undocumented," but not because of any choice she made, I'm not always sure how to judge what is or isn't fair. However, it's not hard to discern what is unjust. It is unjust for a man's family to be punished for his actions, especially when the man in question has been doing righteous work, such as driving an ambulance. It is unjust for a woman to live in fear because she has been acquainted with a clergyman whose biggest crime was an abiding and faithful concern for the poor. It is unjust for a girl to work long hours in grueling conditions in order to support her family, when she should be getting an education. It's unjust to punish the children of undocumented immigrants for the decisions of their parents.

When we do what is just we render to God the things that are God's, and when we submit to unjust human laws we render to Caesar that which is divine. For those who would be guided by the Christian Scriptures while responding to the challenges brought by immigration in the United States, the choice is clear: we must render to God what belongs to God. We must respond with justice. In the next two sections of this book, we'll meet some people—both in government and in the church—who are doing precisely that.

Reflection and Action

Joining the spiritual journey of undocumented immigrants is an act that requires the use of religious imagination. Those who have never migrated across an international border to find work necessary to provide for the basic needs of a family have no direct knowledge of what inspires otherwise rational people to risk their lives in order to cross the U.S./Mexico border in search of a better life.

If we are to assume that migrants who enter and reside in the United States are fellow children of God and, more often than not, fellow Christians, then it behooves us faithfully to engage our imaginations, to consider what it must be like to live the life of an immigrant, and how the life of an immigrant affects the spirit. Through our imaginations, we must engage a migrant spirituality.

The best way to do this is to listen to the stories of immigrants. While we were talking about immigration over coffee at our favorite Portuguese café, Greg Lippman, a friend of mine who is involved in faith-based educational reform in East San José (see chapter 10), and whose parents are Hungarian Jews who immigrated to the United States during the height of the Cold War, talked about immigration in a way that has haunted me as I've written this book.

> Members of my family had to make really difficult choices in order to feed their families—in concentration camps and in Budapest in 1954. My mother lived behind the Iron Curtain and escaped, riding on the underside of a truck while border guards shot at her. Most Americans have no idea what it's like to make such life or death decisions, but I know that if I lived in abject poverty in Mexico and had a chance to move my family to a place where there was a job and educational opportunities for my children and a food bank down the street, I would move. I would have no choice but to move.

The following exercises can be used by individuals or by groups and are meant to help stimulate the imagination as an exercise of compassionate faith.

1. Many immigrants have stories to tell. Listen to those stories and learn them by heart.
2. If you don't have access to the stories of immigrants (or if you are too shy to ask), take stock of all the blessings you enjoy—sufficient income, an overabundance of food, the safety of our homes, and the relative security of our jobs—and then imagine what it would be like to lose the things that keep you secure and make you feel safe. Then imagine a place where some of the good things in life can be restored to you, a place where you can get a job, where your kids can be educated, where health care is available, even if it isn't always affordable. Would you go? What if the journey was hard, dangerous and illegal? Would you still go, if it meant providing a better life for your children?
3. Learn the stories of your own family. Why did they immigrate to the United States (provided you do not come from an American Indian family)? What role did faith have in their decision to

immigrate (provided their immigration was a choice), and how has faith sustained your family's life in the United States?

4. Try reading the Bible imagining how it was understood by your immigrant ancestors or how it may be understood by your immigrant neighbors.

Part 2

Immigration's Political Journey

Chapter 5

Zoe Lofgren and the Politics of Immigration Reform

A nation can be charitable . . . but "charity does not refer only to the institutional or governmental help we give to the "less fortunate." The word means "love." The commandment to "love your enemies" suggests that charity must be without limit; it must include everything. A nation's charity must come from the heart and the imagination of its people. It requires us ultimately to see the world as a community of all the creatures which, to be possessed by any one must be shared by all.

Perhaps that is only a better way of saying that a nation can be civilized. To be civil is to conduct oneself as a responsible citizen, honoring the lives and the rights of others.

—*Wendell Berry*[1]

The offices of the Honorable Zoe Lofgren, a Democrat who represents California's sixteenth district in the United States House of Representatives, sit on the corner of a shaded intersection just north of downtown San José, California in a single-story building that seems to have been intended by its architect—sometime back in the 1970s—to house a dental practice. The congresswoman's staff were friendly—when I stopped by to interview Zoe Lofgren, a cup of coffee was in my hands before my posterior was in a chair, and before the coffee got cold, I knew about one legislative aide's future plans to study social work at a local state college.

This is not, perhaps, what a person might expect when meeting one of the most important and powerful voices for immigration reform in the United States. As chair of the House Judiciary Subcommittee on Immigration, Citizenship, Refugees, Border Security, and International Law (the body within the House of Representatives responsible for immigration reform legislation), Rep. Lofgren was at the center of the immigration reform universe. No one among Washington lawmakers was more knowledgeable about immigration issues, and no one had more power to effect change in American immigration law.

When her chief of staff ushered me into the congresswoman's office, she stood up and introduced herself. "I'm Zoe," she said, extending to me a hand that just days before she had extended to the president of the United States. Then she made sure my coffee mug was refilled, and I thought to myself, "If the immigration reform crafted by this politician reflects any of the warmth, hospitality, and nurture I'm getting in this former dental office, America and her immigrant populations are going to be OK."

After graduating from Stanford in 1970, Zoe Lofgren cut her political teeth working as a congressional aide for Rep. Don Edwards, the congressman who preceded her in California's sixteenth district. During her tenure as an aide she attended and graduated from Santa Clara University Law School, and in 1978 she left politics—briefly—to practice immigration law and teach the subject part-time at Santa Clara University Law School.

When I asked the congresswoman why immigration was such an important issue for her, she told me about her grandfather.

"My grandfather was an immigrant and we were very close. He used to tell me stories about coming over and about the old country, and I've always been interested—I can't tell you why—in the migration of peoples. I remember in elementary school I did a story on the migration of tribes in Africa. I just think it's interesting how the movement of people changes culture."

That interest followed Lofgren into her political life and her legal practice.

"When I worked for my predecessor, Rep. Don Edwards," she told me, "I used to do immigration case work for him, and these are very compelling stories, where people have so much at stake. There are a hundred ways you can run afoul of the law or not understand the law or need assistance, and after I went to law school I practiced immigration law and taught immigration law because, at the time, there were very few people who were doing immigration law and because these cases had all of the excitement, all of the drama of criminal law, except the people involved aren't criminals. It's very compelling."

In the summer of 2009, when Lofgren and I met over coffee in her office, she was optimistic that her lifelong interest in immigration was about to bear fruit in the form of comprehensive immigration reform legislation championed by the White House. She said, "The president told me, 'I will spend any political capital I have left on immigration reform,' and I believe him."

Immigration and the Law: A Thumbnail Sketch

Immigration has been the subject of legislation and lawmaking for almost as long as the United States has had a federal government. The first immigration law, which provided immigrants with a path to citizenship, was enacted in 1790, just a year after the establishment of the United States Constitution,[2] but for the first century of its life the new Republic's immigration policy was one of unconditional welcome. Immigrants poured in from all over the world, and America had no national laws to bar them entrance.[3] By the middle of the nineteenth century, 10 percent of Americans were foreign-born, and immigrants were arriving at a rate of 2.5 million per year.[4]

The Page Act, which was the first federal law restricting immigration, was enacted in 1875, with the stated goal of curtailing the trafficking of prostitutes and forced laborers from "China, Japan and other Oriental countries."[5] The act also excluded those convicted of and serving a sentence for crimes other than political crimes.[6] While the law enacted a prohibition against all human trafficking for the purposes of curbing prostitution and forced labor, it had the intended effect of limiting growth of the Chinese American community because it was assumed that *all* Chinese women were prostitutes.[7]

Soon, the era of restrictive immigration laws was in full swing. In 1882—seven years after the Page Act—President Chester Allen Arthur signed the Chinese Exclusion Act, which barred almost all immigration from China and denied citizenship to Chinese citizens already living in the United States.[8] In 1907, the U.S. government reached an informal agreement with Japan to bar entrance to most Japanese immigrants. And in 1917, Congress passed a law that effectively ended all immigration from Asia and required basic literacy in any language for immigrants over the age of sixteen.[9]

After the chaos and destruction of World War I, American isolationism was in full swing, which greatly affected immigration laws. In 1922, President Harding signed a law enacting immigration quotas based on national origin. Under the Emergency Quota Act, the number of visas extended to each country was set at 3 percent of the total number of people born in that country as recorded in the 1910 census. In other words, if (hypothetically) there were a million Italian-born Americans in the 1910 census, then the government would only approve thirty thousand applications from Italians wanting to immigrate. This law had the effect of sharply decreasing immigration from nations that already had a strong foothold, such as Italy, and almost eliminating immigration from nations that yet had little presence in the United States.

In 1924, the government toughened the standards still further. The quota was revised downward to 2 percent of each immigrant community—based on ethnicity, not upon foreign birth—as measured by the 1890 census, not the 1910 one. Moving the census requirement backward by twenty years effectively curtailed immigration from nations that had seen large spikes in people emigrating to the United States between 1890 and 1910, which was precisely the point. Lawmakers strengthened prohibitions against immigration from Asia and against the naturalization of Asian immigrants already residing in the United States. As a result of the new quota system, immigrants from the British Isles and northern Europe were welcomed almost without restriction since their descendents were already so numerous at the time of the 1890 census, while strict limits were placed upon immigration from eastern and southern Europe.[10]

That 1924 act was the basic standard in American immigration policy for more than forty years, with a few tweaks. In 1952 the McCarran-Walter Act upheld the national quota system, setting the quotas at one-sixth of one percent of each ethnic group based upon the 1920 census. The quota system was changed, however. Now it allowed those with desirable skills to move to the head of the line, and it opened the door to immigration from Asia—just a crack—with a minimum of one hundred visas issued annually to each Asian country.[11] And in 1965, the government passed the Hart-Celler Act, which drastically changed American immigration law by abolishing national immigration quotas and by facilitating family unification by allowing foreign-born residents to sponsor the immigration of family members. The Hart-Celler Act allowed for the immigration of people from all over the world, and as such it, perhaps more than any other legislation, has helped to shape a modern America blessed with the diversity we enjoy.

Since 1965, the United States' immigration laws have been amended to adjust the number of immigrants admitted (in 1976, 1978, and 1990), to provide for the welcoming of refugees (1980), and to extend amnesty to undocumented immigrants (1986);[12] in 1997 President Clinton signed a bill mandating stricter enforcement of immigration laws. These last two laws were targeted specifically at undocumented migrants from Mexico, the subject to which we turn next.

Twentieth-Century Immigration from Mexico

During the first three decades of the twentieth century, the limits on immigration from Asia and from southern and eastern Europe had the effect of increasing northward migration across the U.S./Mexico border. As laborers from Asia and from southern and eastern Europe became scarce due to a lack of fresh immigration from those countries, labor-intensive industries such as agriculture, mining, and the railroads turned, increasingly, to Mexico as a source of inexpensive, unskilled labor. The need for Mexican labor became acute during the First World War, when the United States supplied the European Allies and, later, its own armed forces with cotton for uniforms, copper for bullet casings, and food for hungry soldiers.

At the same time, conditions in Mexico encouraged northward migration. The economic policies of Mexico during the twenty-four-year-long dictatorship of the Mexican general Porfirio Díaz accentuated the contrast between Mexico's wealthy and impoverished classes, and the ranks of Mexico's poor swelled. Between 1910 and 1920 the Mexican Revolution and, a few years later, the Cristero

Wars threw the nation into a prolonged season of violence from which hundreds of thousands of refugees fled. Many of these escaped across the U.S./Mexico border, where agricultural and industrial jobs supporting the war effort awaited them.[13]

This is not to say that Mexicans migrated north without arousing resistance among the Americans of European descent. In 1917 and again in 1922, as American laws placed restriction on immigration from Asia and parts of Europe, many American lawmakers also attempted to limit immigration from Mexico. Powerful agricultural and industrial interests opposed these efforts, however, and the legislators' attempts failed, as did a pair of bills introduced in Congress in 1925 and 1926 that would have established a quota system limiting Mexican immigration. In 1924, the United States Justice Department established the Border Patrol, an act that was symbolic at best—in its early years, the Border Patrol was meant to patrol the two thousand miles of border with just 450 officers.[14]

The Great Depression ushered in a new era in the history of immigration and the relationship between the United States and Mexico. As the United States' economy contracted and jobs became scarce, immigration enforcement along the border was increased, and the United States began forcibly to repatriate both Mexican citizens and those mistaken for Mexican citizens. In all, repatriations sent more than half a million people to Mexico. As many as half were American citizens.[15] Ironically, this crackdown happened at a time when fewer Mexicans were immigrating to the United States because of the dismal economy and lack of jobs here. Even though so many Mexicans returned home voluntarily, those that remained were often blamed for the loss of American jobs, resulting in forced repatriation.

With the outbreak of World War II, the United States once more needed a steady supply of labor, and in 1942 the United States and Mexico signed an agreement allowing for the temporary and seasonal migration of Mexican citizens into the United States. Often called the Bracero[16] program, the agreement between the two neighboring nations, with a few revisions, lasted for twenty-two years, during which hundreds of thousands of workers migrated across the border annually, primarily to work on America's industrial farms.

The Bracero Program certainly wasn't a perfect system, and it was not accepted by everyone. Many Americans felt as if the system was being abused as a way for Mexicans to enter the United States without any intention of returning to Mexico. In 1952, while the Bracero era was well underway, the United States Attorney General ordered a massive deportation of undocumented immigrants called "Operation Wetback," which, within the space of a few short years, oversaw the deportation and repatriation of 3.7 million undocumented migrants.[17] As with the systematic Depression-era deportations, many of the deported actually were American citizens.

It is interesting to note that part of the motivation behind Operation Wetback was a fear that Communist subversives were entering the United States in the guise of undocumented workers. With the clear vision of historical hindsight we now know that this was McCarthy-era paranoia. It would be easy to make light of the naive hysteria behind Operation Wetback, except that as the first decade of the twenty-first century draws to a close, many of those who continue to call for strict enforcement along the U.S./Mexico border do so motivated, in part, by a desire to keep Al Qaeda operatives and other Islamist terrorists off American soil. It's a different era with a new paranoia, but it's also clear that some habits are hard to break.

In recent years there have been several attempts to alter immigration law significantly in one way or another, but for the most part, changes to American immigration law and policy have been incremental, unfocused, cumbersome, and confusing. The United States' immigration laws are a system in need of reform, but reforming the system is difficult. Zoe Lofgren is fond of saying, "If immigration reform were easy, it would have happened already."

The Future of Immigration Reform

When the American people elected Barack Obama as President of the United States in 2008, many did so, in part, because they were attracted by his campaign promise to enact sweeping immigration reform. Six months into his first term, Barack Obama started work on immigration reform by calling together a bipartisan group of House, Senate, and administration leaders for a summit on immigration reform. After the meeting, Zoe Lofgren issued a hopeful assessment of their prospects:

> I'm heartened that President Obama shares my desire to push forward with a bipartisan comprehensive immigration reform bill. As I've stated before, Congress cannot move this legislation without the President's active involvement and support. Today's meeting reinforced my hope that we can pass a bipartisan and comprehensive bill that ensures our borders are secure, that our laws are enforced, that promotes family values with family unification, that regularizes the status of those that currently live in the shadows, that protects American workers, and provides for the legitimate needs of our economy.[18]

When we met, I asked Congresswoman Lofgren to tell me more about the goals for immigration reform that she enumerated in the statement she made after her meeting with the president.

"People are frustrated," she told me, "that laws are not being respected. People feel as if the law should be followed. *I* feel as if the law should be followed. Now, some laws are impossible to enforce, and that's where reform comes in, but you have to lead with an assurance that the law will be upheld, otherwise you will get nowhere."

The idea that immigration reform should reflect "family values" and keep families united is of particular importance to Lofgren. It's also one of the most divisive issues on the table in Washington.

Those who oppose immigration reform—and those who want to see immigration policy reformed so that it is more restrictive—often express concern over the fact that United States law allows undocumented immigrants to give birth to American citizens, so long as those children are born on American soil, because the United States Constitution confers the privileges of citizenship upon everyone born in the United States or its territories. In its more draconian moments, the enforcement of U.S. immigration law has attempted to discourage undocumented persons from procreating on U.S. soil by deporting the undocumented parents of U.S. citizen children. Lofgren hopes this will change.

"We say we believe in supporting families. Meanwhile we're deporting mothers and separating them from their little children. How is that supporting family values? Or we have people who are legal residents of the United States, who have followed all of the rules, and we separate them from their spouses for four or five years. How is that promoting family values? I don't think it is."

Equally difficult to achieve will be Lofgren's goal of regularizing those who live in the shadows by providing them with a path to legal residency. For those who oppose her kind of immigration reform, such regularization amounts to an amnesty for immigrants who have broken American laws, a tacit approval of disregard for the order of law. Amnesty, or anything looking like it, is a hot button for the vocal and politically savvy community of Americans who oppose immigration reform.

For Lofgren, however, regularizing the status of undocumented immigrants is an issue to be dealt with pragmatically. It's not a matter of letting millions of new immigrants into the country; rather, it's about dealing with the fact that millions of undocumented immigrants are already here, already working. If they are mistreated by their employers or paid below the minimum wage, they cannot complain or seek redress.

"When an employer mistreats his workers, that undercuts his competitors who are playing by [the] rules," said Lofgren. "It benefits no one. It just needs to be changed, both for the workers and for those who are playing by the rules.

"This is why I've said I want immigration reform that protects American workers: you cannot have a scheme that protects the wages, hours, and working conditions of American workers, and yet have a segment of the population that is a free-fire zone. The best way to make sure that the labor conditions of American workers—which I take very seriously—are not undercut is to make sure that everyone plays by the same rules, and you cannot do that without codifying the shadow workforce."

The idea that the "shadow workforce" should be brought into the open strikes fear into a certain segment of the American population. The fear is that providing amnesty for undocumented workers will serve to encourage more undocumented migration.

Lofgren is undaunted by such suggestions. When I asked her about how immigration policy might meet the legitimate needs of the American economy, she asked me a question: "Do you know how many visas are allocated for non-skilled workers each year?" I didn't.

"Five thousand!" She delivered the number like the punch line of a joke. "And we have more than a million agriculture workers, 70 to

80 percent of whom are undocumented, and we only have five thousand visas. Did we create this situation? Yes. To issue five thousand visas a year for unskilled labor is absurd. We need to have a realistic assessment of the role immigrants play in building up the American economy and allow for the regular movement of people to meet that economic need."

When asked what role the religious community can play in the process of achieving comprehensive immigration reform that "ensures our borders are secure, that our laws are enforced, that promotes family values with family unification, that regularizes the status of those that currently live in the shadows, that protects American workers, and provides for the legitimate needs of our economy," Lofgren complimented the work of Catholic and mainline Protestant lobbyists, but as she reflected on matters of faith her comments took us away from public policy.

> You can't, as a minister or priest, tell your congregation what to think on a political question—it's resented in America if you try to do so, and rightly so. But how one treats one's neighbor is, in fact, a proper subject, and I think some of the vitriolic hatred that has occurred around immigration—whether or not your parishioners are going to agree with you that immigration laws should be reformed—it should not be acceptable that there be hate or the kind of dismissive attitude toward immigrants. We've had a rise in hate crime, especially toward Latinos, that, I think, is very much related to the immigration debate. I think, in addition to the organized advocacy, to bring the temperature down so that people can be civil to each other is an extremely important role.

Fair enough.

Before I met with the congresswoman, as I sat in the reception area of her office, drinking coffee and chatting with a friendly legislative aide, I noticed a common garden snail crawling up the inside of the front door. The aide and I had a laugh about invasive molluscoid interlopers as I threw the snail into the bushes outside the office. As I left through the same door through which I had sent the snail, I was gratified to know that our nation's immigration policy is, in large part, in the hands of someone who doesn't see immigrants as human snails—invasive pests who consume more than they contribute.

I've always felt the church is at its best when it regards politicians with a prophetic suspicion—assuming they will be corrupted by power and will not place the needs of the poor and powerless above the demands of corporate greed. But sitting in that renovated dentist's office, drinking coffee with Zoe Lofgren, it felt possible that the halls of American power may be infused with a tincture of the spirit of Toribio Romo.

Chapter 6

The Busiest (and Kindest) Federal Judge in America

President Reagan, who was in favor of strong borders, once remarked that "a nation without borders is not really a nation," but he constantly reminded us that America must remain a "beacon" and a "shining city on a hill" for immigrants who continually renew our great country with their energy and add to the nation's economic growth and prosperity.

Americans and immigrants share the same values of work, family and opportunity. There is no reason to fear the newcomers arriving on our shores today. If anything, they will energize what is best about our country.

The only way to realize America's vision is through comprehensive immigration reform legislation.

—*Jack Kemp*[1]

When I visited the federal courthouse in Las Cruces, New Mexico, I had two initial reactions. The first was amazement at the way in which American architects of a certain era seemed so unable to produce beautiful public buildings, for in Las Cruces the laws of the United States are adjudicated in what looks like a three-story cinderblock with windows. It is an architectural style that may charitably be called "Cold War Boring." My second response was one of relief when I saw that a new courthouse is being built. The new structure will be much larger and infinitely more interesting. Thank goodness.

I was in Las Cruces to meet a man who has been called "the busiest federal judge in the United States,"[2] the Honorable Robert C.

Brack, United States District Judge for the United States District Court of Las Cruces, New Mexico. He may be America's busiest judge, but the workload doesn't seem to have broken his spirit. I would not at all be surprised if Judge Brack is also the kindest judge in the United States.

I made my way into the building, through an airport-like security checkpoint past which visitors are not allowed to take cameras or recording devices (my iPhone, a critical device in the writing of this book, is both—ouch!) and up to the third floor, where I sat in the back of Judge Brack's courtroom to watch him sentence inmates charged with crimes related to immigration. On the day I was in Judge Brack's courtroom the accused sat in the jury box, which was oddly appropriate, since they all acted as their own juries by pleading guilty to the offenses for which they were accused. They were chained by their hands and feet and wore green and sometimes orange jailhouse garments.

Ten defendants—nine Mexicans and a Guatemalan—went before the judge on that Friday morning beginning at eight-thirty. Each was charged with criminal reentry without inspection, meaning that they had been deported previously and had been caught trying to get back into the United States. After pleading guilty, each was sentenced to time served in jail—usually between three and six weeks—and all but one left the court with orders for deportation. The other claimed to be a legal resident of Oregon; the judge sent his case to an immigration judge in El Paso.

The defendants stood before the judge one at a time, beside court-appointed defense lawyers. Judge Brack talked to them about their families and about what motivated them repeatedly to cross the border. As he spoke he smiled, looking each person in the eyes, making a human connection before handing down his sentence.

"I hope you find work at home that pays you a just wage," he told several of the defendants, and to each he gave a warning against reentry. "It used to be that you could come across the border and you could return voluntarily and without consequence, but those days are over. If I see you back into this courtroom I will have no choice but to send you to jail for at least a year."

To a man sentenced to return home to his wife and six children in Juárez, the Mexican city closest to Las Cruces, he said, "I'm happy to tell you that you will be home this afternoon. You need to go home. Your wife has her hands full with six children who need their father. I admire your efforts on behalf of your family, and I don't fault you for what you have done. *Vaya con Dios.* Go with God."

Then the judge asked the father of six if he had anything he wanted to say to the court.

"*Solo quiero decirle gracias, y que Dios le bendiga.*" (I just want to say thank you, and may God bless you.)

"Thank you for blessing me," responded the judge. "I'm excited that you will soon be back with your family."

To the only Guatemalan on the day's docket the judge said, "I see in your paperwork that your wife's name is Milagro. It's my favorite name for a female. It means 'miracle.' Go back to her."

The judge asked Milagro's husband how he had traveled from his native Guatemala to the United States along the length of Mexico, and he was relieved when he found out that the young man had not ridden on the top of a freight train, as many migrants from Central America do. He warned against riding rails hobo-style and he asked the man if he thought he might be able to find work in Guatemala.

"I couldn't say," came the reply.

"I know it must be a desperate situation that makes a young husband and father leave his family," said the judge. "I pray that you will find work so that you won't have to leave again. *Vaya con Dios.* Go with God."

"*Gracias a Dios, y a usted.*" Thanks be to God and to you.

The penultimate defendant that morning, besides crossing the border without inspection and without papers, also was facing a charge of drunk driving. It is an offense for which Judge Brack could have assigned a harsher penalty, but, like the others, the jail sentence handed down was for time already served. Like the others, the man with a DUI was deported. This time, the sentencing came with a stern warning. "It appears that you have a problem with alcohol. It is a demon that knows no borders. My own father was an alcoholic and fifteen years before he died he was delivered from that demon. I know there is a power able to deliver you. For the sake of your family I hope you will be delivered."

The final defendant, the man from Oregon whose case was referred to an immigration court in El Paso, used the judge's offer of an opportunity to speak to the court to express what must certainly have been on the minds of his fellow defendants. "Thank you, Your Honor. When we spend time in jail together we become kinda like a family, you know? And we need to hear what you have to say. You're kinda like, I don't know, a brother or a father or a grandfather to us."

And with that the defendants shuffled out of the jury box accompanied by the jingle of chains that would fall off their wrists and ankles as soon as they crossed the border and headed south toward home.

As I sat watching the proceedings and listening to the words that were spoken in the courtroom, it felt a lot like church. Both the judge and the defendants evoked the name of God and God's Spirit felt present. I also shed a few tears, and hoped that the court would not be disturbed by my sniffling as I sat on a bench that looked for all the world like a pew pilfered from a decommissioned desert church. As much as I think the new courthouse building will be an improvement over the old one, I hope the pews follow Judge Brack into his new digs.

Building Compassion for Immigrants

The day before I visited Judge Brack's courtroom, I met with him in his chambers. I asked him to reflect on how his faith informs his work as a federal judge who must enforce immigration laws and policies enacted by politicians.

"It's a fair question," he said, and he looked out one of his chambers' windows, which frame the Organ Mountains east of Las Cruces. "I've been a Christian my whole life. I was raised in the Catholic Church, and I remain a Catholic. I don't find that faith is something I can compartmentalize, and faith has tenderized my heart toward everyone I meet. I pray for wisdom every day before I go into my courtroom."

He looked out the window some more.

> Six years ago, when I came here, I knew nothing of immigration. I had no sense of its history or nuance. I was a state district court judge in Clovis, New Mexico. Immigration is a federal issue, I wasn't living along the border, and my opinions, like those of

> most Americans, were formed by what I was getting in the media. I'm a George W. Bush appointee, and if you had asked me about immigration back then I would have had the kind of response you might expect from a Bush appointee. "You need to enforce immigration laws as a matter of national sovereignty. Laws have to be enforced. Stronger enforcement will deter immigration."
>
> I had been here about a week when a border patrol agent was being cross-examined in my courtroom, and the lawyer asked him to describe the "V.R." or "voluntary return" program. I had no idea what the V.R. program was, but the agent described it by saying that when they apprehend someone crossing the border they offer to let that person sign a voluntary return form and they drive the migrant back to the border and walk him across without charging him with a crime.
>
> So I asked him how many times they would do a voluntary return before they charged the migrant with a crime, and the answer was "fifteen." I laughed out loud on the bench. I mean, if you don't think the Voluntary Return policy isn't asking for people to attempt to cross illegally. . . .

Judge Brack cocked his head, raised his eyebrows and squinted one eye.

> Of course they come across. If they try to cross the border there are three possible outcomes, and only one is bad. They can die trying to cross, which is bad, but mostly they don't. Mostly they either make it across, which is good, or they get a free ride back to the border where they can try again to cross the border, and they know nothing will happen to them. That's good too, but here's the thing: after letting folks go back and try again to cross fifteen times, on the sixteenth time, we charge them with a felony attempt to reenter, and they end up in my courtroom, where I have to sentence them as felons."

In six years on the federal bench Judge Brack has averaged 100 felony sentencings per month. Most federal district judges average about seventy-five felonies per year. During five of his six years as a federal district judge he has had more felony convictions than any other federal judge, and 95 percent of them are immigration-related—felony reentry or for the use of false documents. In the month before I met him, at a time when the American media reported a decline in border crossings, Judge Brack sentenced two hundred and fifty people with felony reentry.

When we talked, Judge Brack estimated that he had heard seven thousand stories during his tenure as a federal district judge, and, while he's never heard the same story twice, he finds that those who tell their stories tend to fit similar profiles. First, there is the parent who wants to find a job to support his family in Mexico.

"I look at these guys and they take their role as husband, as father, as provider seriously," he told me. "There's no work in Mexico, so these men do the same thing their fathers did. It's the same thing their grandfathers and even great-grandfathers did. They come north to where the jobs are.

"Then there's the guy who was brought to the United States by his parents when he was maybe four years old. He grew up here and went to high school and married a cheerleader. He is, in every way, an American, except that maybe he gets stopped for what should be a traffic ticket and he doesn't have a license, because he's here illegally, and he gets deported. Our guys pick him up and take him across the bridge in Juárez, and he's never been to Mexico before. Maybe he doesn't even speak Spanish. He's got no prospect for a job. He doesn't know anyone. So what do you think he's going to do? Of course he's going to attempt to cross back into the States, only for him it's a felony if he gets caught.

"I had a guy like that in my court the other day, and he spoke eloquently, in perfect English. He asked me if I'm a father, which I am. He then asked me if I got to see my children take their first steps, or if I heard them speak their first words. I had. 'And that's all I want,' he told me, and how does one husband and father say to another husband and father, 'I'm sorry, I have to send you away from your family?'"

Judge Brack looked out the window again, his eyes noticeably moist.

> Then there's the kid who comes from somewhere in central Mexico who's got nothing, except he's got a dream. He wants to make something of himself so he heads north and he gets to the border and he cannot afford a *coyote*, but there are always people willing to show him how to get across if he'll take a backpack of mari-

> juana on his back. All this kid has is hope, so he takes the backpack and he gets caught with a backpack full of marijuana. Now he doesn't even have hope.
>
> Not long ago I had two young men from Oaxaca who didn't even speak Spanish. They spoke Mixtec, and we had to get a translator. It turns out that there was a crop failure in their village, and the village got together, pooled their resources, and sent these young men north in the hope that they could make money to provide for the economic needs of the village.
>
> They went north on the back of a train, and by bus 'til they got to the border, and when they got to the border they had nothing. Well, they got caught, and in my courtroom they said they'd go back into Mexico and not attempt a return, if that's what I wanted, but then they had to return to their village with the knowledge that they'd let the whole village down. They lost the hope of their entire village.

"God has given me the grace to empathize," Judge Brack told me.

Amnesty and the Future of Reform

In 2006 and 2007 there was an attempt in Washington to improve immigration law. Known as the Comprehensive Immigration Reform Act of 2007, or informally as the "Kennedy-McCain Bill," the proposed law, among other things, would have provided for a guest worker program for those employed in low-skilled, low-paying jobs, and which would have given undocumented immigrants living in the United States a path to legal residency. The bill included provisions designed to keep families intact and to improve economic conditions in Mexico.[3]

While lawmakers on Capitol Hill were negotiating the details of the Kennedy-McCain Bill, Judge Brack called Senator Pete Domenici, then the senior senator from New Mexico, and a friend of the judge's. He told the senator about his experiences adjudicating federal immigration law and gave some suggestions for how the laws might be improved. Several of his suggestions ended up in the Kennedy-McCain Bill. Had the bill passed, many of the people I saw in Judge Brack's courtroom would have been at work that morning, earning a living and providing for their families, but the politicians in Washington didn't have the political will to pass the bill. "I've sentenced more than three thousand people since the Kennedy-McCain Bill failed," he told me with palpable disappointment, "all of them felonies."

When we spoke in the summer of 2009, Judge Brack was pessimistic when I asked him about the prospects for immigration reform legislation. "The agenda is being controlled by misinformation and by xenophobes in Washington," he told me. "Meanwhile, we're asking these terribly poor people to bear the brunt of a broken policy.

"People tell me that amnesty is a bad idea because it just rewards law-breakers, and I ask, what do you think our current policy with voluntary return does? Sometimes we apprehend and repatriate people twice in the same day. How is that not encouraging people to break the law?

"Then people will say we should send illegal immigrants to the back of the line because people all over the world are waiting for the opportunity legally to immigrate to the United States, and why should a Mexican be given preference over a Pole or someone from another country? Well, the answer is that we have a special relationship with Mexico. The border between our two countries is the border with the greatest contrast of economies in the whole world. Here we have the world's largest superpower next door to a third-world country and we in the United States have grown used to having Mexico as a supply of cheap labor. The economics are easy to understand. It's all supply and demand. We don't have that kind of relationship with other countries."

More than anything, Judge Robert Brack of the Federal District Court in Las Cruces, New Mexico, wants people to know the truth about immigration. "I fear the debate doesn't take into account what I see," he told me. "The people I see are not criminals, and they're not looking for a handout. They are mothers and fathers trying to feed their children. If people knew what I see, then maybe it would counter negative stereotypes so that compassionate and humane immigration laws could be passed in Washington."

It's worth noting that Judge Brack is a man who is not easy to categorize. He has detractors who think he's too lenient ("If you add an extra 'a' to my name it becomes "'Barack,'" he joked), but Judge

Brack is hardly a liberal, at least not in the way most Americans use the term. As we spoke together, and as his eyes rested on the view of the mountains outside his window, my eyes tended to wander to the bookshelf behind him. There, among photos of his family, I spotted a book by Robert Bork and a photo of Judge Brack standing with Supreme Court Justice Antonin Scalia. Judge Brack recently had been fishing with Justice Scalia, a man who, it could be argued, is among the most conservative Supreme Court justices of his generation. As far as I've been able to tell, Judge Brack's nonimmigration decisions are typical of a Bush-the-Younger appointee.[4] Yet his faith and his experience adjudicating immigration law have led Judge Brack away from a traditionally conservative perspective on and approach to immigration issues.

Judge Brack, however, seems comfortable outside of conventional labels. He told me that at his Senate confirmation hearing, Senator Lindsey Graham of South Carolina, then the chair of the Senate Judicial Committee, asked him about his judicial philosophy. Was he an "activist" or a "strict constructionist"? Judge Brack chose to eschew those labels—which he doesn't like anyway. Instead he quoted the prophet Micah:

> He has told you, O mortal, what is good:
> and what does the Lord require of you
> but to do justice, and to love kindness,
> and to walk humbly with your God?
> (Mic. 6:8)

I asked Judge Brack how his work affected him personally and spiritually. He claimed to be unaffected by his work on a daily basis and said he was able to go home happy each afternoon, but he admitted to having a harder time relaxing on vacation. The positive effects of time away wear off quickly these days, due to what he describes as "the unrelenting tragedy and sadness" he encounters in his work.

"I know God put me here for a reason," he told me, and surely that must sustain him somewhat. Then there's his window. As we talked Judge Brack looked out the window a lot, and I know that if it were my job to sit on Judge Brack's bench and to inhabit his chambers, I'd look out that window too. It's a good view, and more than being beautiful it calls to mind the words of the Psalmist:

I lift up my eyes to the hills—
from where will my help come?
My help comes from the Lord,
who made heaven and earth.
(Ps. 121:1–2)

Reflection and Action

For me, the morning of Saturday, August 8, 2009 was happy. I was enjoying the end of three weeks of paid vacation from my work as a Presbyterian minister. My eighteen-year-old Burmese foster daughter had just rejoined the family after spending more than a month away from home honing her English language skills at a private boarding school. The kids and I slept in while my wife enjoyed a morning workout at the local YMCA. I made waffles with my children; they argued about who got to fold the egg whites into the batter and bickered over rights to the first waffle off the iron.

After breakfast I took my two youngest kids to a soccer class at the Y, where they played their first actual game of soccer (until then the class had been entirely dedicated to fostering basic skills). My five-year-old daughter showed some real promise as a midfielder and she scored her team's only goal. My four-year-old son collapsed in tears because the opposing team wouldn't share the ball with him.

When we got home, the kids ate leftover Chinese food for lunch and had a water balloon fight with friends from the neighborhood.

The day wasn't perfect, but it was good, and it was infused with the kind of happiness for which I would cross a dozen borders without permission. I think that's true for most of us. The ingredients for the good life I enjoy in San José, California—employment that pays more than a living wage, plenty of food, educational and recreational opportunities for my children, and the freedom to watch my daughter score her first goal—are readily available to most people living in the United States; almost everyone who crosses our nation's borders illegally wants these things too.

On that August day, I reflected upon the people I have met during my years of spiritual journeying with immigrants, and about how, more than anything else, happiness is the motivation for crossing a border, with or without papers. Often, this happiness is pursued economically and sometimes happiness is seen as a life safe from war or other forms of violence, but I've never met anyone whose pursuit of happiness wasn't legitimate. Migrants seek the same happiness I enjoyed on the morning my family ate waffles and my kids played soccer. This is not a happiness that is free of complication, or a happiness of cheap thrills. It is a deep happiness that is rich and textured and full of life.

For Christians who believe that the pursuit of happiness is an inalienable right, endowed upon humanity by a benevolent Creator, the following actions seem natural and worthy of our consideration. These actions can be taken by individuals or by groups.

1. Recognize the pursuit of happiness in the lives of your immigrant neighbors.
2. If you are a citizen, celebrate that privilege by being active. Write to your legislators. Send letters to the editor of your local newspaper. Blog and tweet and have Facebook interactions till justice rolls down like waters and righteousness like a broadband Internet connection. Advocate for immigration reform that keeps families united and that recognizes the economic needs both north and south of the border. Fight any legislation that demonizes immigrants or criminalizes acts of mercy, compassion, and charity.
3. Never assume that immigration is a "liberal" or "progressive" issue. Chapter six began with an epigraph from Jack Kemp, who hardly was an icon of the American Left; Judge Robert Brack, who may possess the nation's most eloquent legal voice for immigration reform, is a George W. Bush appointee who goes fishing with Antonin Scalia. (And to be entirely fair, it should also be noted that George W. Bush had a relatively immigrant-friendly record as governor of Texas.)

As we've seen, the best way to understand immigrants' situations is to listen to their stories. The third and final section of this book tells the stories of immigrants who are pursuing happiness and of individuals and institutions who respond to that pursuit with compassion and hospitality. What are Christians doing to extend hospitality to immigrant neighbors? What can *you* do?

Part 3

Father Toribio Rides Again

Chapter 7

Frontera de Cristo

> *From the viewpoint of faith, the motive which in the last instance moves Christians to participate in the liberation of oppressed peoples and exploited social classes is the conviction of the radical incompatibility of evangelical demands with an unjust, alienating society. They feel keenly that they cannot claim to be Christians without a commitment to liberation. But the articulation of the way in which this action for a more just world is related to a life of faith belongs to a level of intuition and groping—at times in anguish.*
>
> *Gustavo Gutiérrez*[1]

The late afternoon wind blew strong, whipping up dust and making me fear for my hat, which I still needed against the sun as it came to rest on the mountain peaks west of town. I was standing in a McDonald's parking lot in Douglas, Arizona, a border town about two hours' drive south of Tucson. This McDonald's isn't the first fast food joint you come to if you cross the U.S./Mexico border and drive north from Agua Prieta, Sonora—that distinction is held by the Carl's Junior across the street—but it's close enough to the border to welcome those coming north to the home of everything that is super-sized.

I made the trip south and east from my home in California's Silicon Valley to become acquainted with the work of *Frontera de Cristo*, a binational Presbyterian ministry working with migrants on both sides of the border that divides not just two nations, but also a single community—Douglas, Arizona in the north and Agua Prieta, Sonora in the south.

Six weeks before arriving in Douglas, I had called the offices of *Frontera de Cristo* to see if I might pay them a visit. I spoke with Mark Adams, a Presbyterian minister from South Carolina who runs *Frontera de Cristo*, together with Angel Valencia, a Presbyterian lay pastor and former businessman from Chihuahua. With a gentle southern drawl, Mark told me, "You'll want to come on a Tuesday. That's when we have our prayer vigil, which is kind of the heart of our ministry to migrants."

Six weeks later, on a Tuesday, I was in Douglas ready to pray.

Lift High the Cross: Praying for the Immigrant Dead

Ten of us gathered for the vigil: me, three *Frontera de Cristo* staff members, a couple of regulars from the community, and four volunteers with a Tucson-based organization called "No More Deaths," which, among other things, leaves water and supplies in the desert in an effort to save the lives of those making the dangerous journey through the desert north into the United States while evading the Border Patrol. Participants in the vigil arrived on bikes and by car. One of the regulars rode up on a late-model Harley.

A member of the *Frontera de Cristo* staff, Tommy Basset (about whom we'll learn more later), came to the McDonald's parking lot in a green, four-wheel-drive pickup whose bed was filled with several dozen crosses fashioned from white one-by-twos. Each cross was about two feet high, and each bore the name of a migrant who had died trying to cross the border in Cochise County, Arizona.

We each took an armload of crosses and made our way across the street separating McDonald's and Carl's Junior, to a place where there is a small monument honoring the first person who is known to have died crossing the border near Douglas and Agua Prieta. The vigil began with a time of accommodating silence. Spiritually, it was an eclectic group: some Presbyterians and Roman Catholics, some Unitarians, a Quaker or two. The guy on the Harley seemed to have embraced a Native American spirituality, and Tommy, the guy with the crosses, described his own religious background to me by saying, "I was brought up Roman Catholic and wandered around through Evangelical churches and hung out with the Presbyterians and the

Episcopalians and the Buddhists. Now I kind of consider myself a 'Cathoterian' who is into the Virgin of Guadalupe and loves Zen meditation—a smorgasbord."

After the silence, the vigil began. We walked out to the street that leads to the border crossing and made our way south toward Mexico. One by one we held our crosses high in the air, looked to the north and yelled the name written on the crossbeam. "*¡Raúl Martinez Hernandez!*" perhaps, or "*¡Maria Garcia de la Vega!*" After the shouting of each name, the gathered crowed responded "*¡Presente!*" Present. Then we laid the crosses against the curb next to the sidewalk on the street that leads into Mexico.

The third time it was my turn to shout the name of someone who had died crossing the border, I looked at the cross in my hand and saw, instead of a name, the words "*no identificado.*" Not identified. It caught me off guard. Stifling the rising emotions, I lifted the cross and mispronounced the words "*no identificado.*" In that moment, I became aware that someone close by was listening to Michael Jackson singing "Billy Jean" on an automotive stereo, perhaps while waiting in the Carl's Junior drive-thru. At the time, Michael Jackson had been dead only a few weeks. The king of Pop's music was everywhere that summer, as people remembered the life of a great, if deeply flawed, artist. In that moment the importance of the vigil came into focus for me as I held up a cross in honor and in memory of an anonymous person—a young woman in my imagination—whose life had expired somewhere in the sands of the desert under the blank and pitiless sun, her flesh, no doubt, made food for indignant desert birds. Whereas Michael Jackson's voice was ubiquitous in the summer of his death, played endlessly on every kind of entertainment device, we were singing the songs of those whose voices went silent and of whom the world took no notice.

The cross I lifted up—like all of the crosses held high that day—honored the image of God that once infused the living body of someone who was a daughter certainly, and perhaps a lover, a mother or a sister, probably a friend. Whatever her relationships in life, in death this anonymous child of God was the victim of an international border, of economic realities that drive people to seek a better life in a forbidden land, and of fearful policies and laws enacted by politicians who are removed from the geography and the people whose motives they choose not to understand. She died a victim of those who don't remember, who cannot remember her lest they be confronted with the enormity of the injustice that is manifest when "the best lack all conviction and the worst are filled with passionate intensity."[2]

To call out the memory of someone who died in anonymity and to declare her present is to engage in a reckoning that humanizes both the deceased and the timid individual standing on a dusty street in an unfamiliar town holding up a cross while a boyish voice declares that he is not the father of Billy Jean's kid. To declare the unnamed dead present is to affirm that common humanity ought to transcend a shared border.

As our slow and solemn procession of remembering wended its way down the last yards of American territory, we were joined by the curious and the late. A grandmother brought three grandchildren with her. A few cars honked in support. A Border Patrol agent driving a K-9 unit pickup truck gave us a quizzical look through the dusty, tinted glass of his driver's side window. A man on a bicycle with a thick Mexican accent cursed the "Wetbacks" and "Illegals" and the "goddamn U.S. government" who wasn't doing anything about them. He pedaled past us, cussing as he disappeared across the border into Mexico.[3] I am not sure what his issue was with illegal immigrants, but it's clear that passion runs high on this issue on both sides of the border.

At the end of our southbound procession we formed a circle in the last wide spot before the border. We spent more time in silent prayer and then passed the remaining three crosses, from person to person, around the circle. By this time our group had grown to fifteen. Each person was invited to hold the cross for a time, to pray over it, to be blessed by the memory of the one whose name was inscribed on its crosspiece. As the crosses made their way around the circle we each offered our prayers silently; the man who rode a Harley lifted each cross, holding it up to the four winds. Then he stood each cross on the ground, lightly tapping it, connecting it with the earth before blessing it, removing it, and handing it to me.

My interaction with the crosses and with the memory of those lives they represented was that of a pastor in the Calvinist tradition. Silently, I offered up the committal prayer I offer when I preside at the funeral of a member of my congregation:

Into your hands, O Merciful Savior,
We commend the spirit of our brother Juan
(or our sister Carmen, or the unnamed brother or sister remembered here),
A lamb of our own flock,
A sheep of your own fold,
Receive him (or her) into the arms of your mercy,
Into the blessed rest of everlasting peace,
And in the glorious company of the saints of light.
Amen.

The LORD gives and the LORD takes away.
Blessed be the name of the LORD.

We shared prayers and reflections and the vigil closed with a chorus whose lyrics were adapted from Psalm 104:

Envia su Espíritu Santo;
Sea renovada la faz de la tierra.
(Send your Holy Spirit;
May the face of the earth be renewed.)

We walked back to McDonald's, picking up the crosses we had left. We deposited them in milk crates in Tommy's truck where they would remain until the following Tuesday. Then, once more, they would stand in prophetic witness to the resurrection of human memory, and to the everlasting life of those whose souls are at rest in the loving arms of a God who never forgets.

Welcoming the Stranger

I left my car at McDonald's and crossed the border into Mexico with Mark Adams. Together with the Roman Catholic Church in Agua Prieta, *Frontera de Cristo* runs a resource center for recently deported migrants. I was scheduled to volunteer at the center that night, but first I ate dinner with Mark's family at their home in Agua Prieta.

Mark has a lovely family. His wife, Miriam, is from Chiapas, a state in southern Mexico famous for its coffee and its civil unrest. Their three children—thirteen, five, and two—were full of life. We ate *chili colorado* with rice, beans, and tortillas; we drank water made wonderful with lime and mint. The heat of the evening grew humid and it rained with lightning and thunder and wind.

After dinner, as we drove to the migrant resource center, I asked Mark what inspired him to leave South Carolina in favor of Sonora. "It's a good question," he replied.

"If you had told me I would be where I am today in high school or even in college I'd have laughed in your face. I was active in my church back home, but even though people told me I'd make a good preacher, I didn't want to be a pastor. I told folks that I was going to serve the kingdom of God by being a high school Spanish teacher."

After college Mark signed up to be a short-time mission volunteer for one of Presbyterian Border Ministry's mission sites that spans Eagle Pass, Texas and Piedras Negras, Coahuila. The experience changed him. "I was converted by the people in Mexico," he told me.

Mark went back to Clover, South Carolina to teach Spanish at the high school from which he had graduated, but he couldn't get Mexico out of his mind. He quit his job, went to seminary and, upon graduation, found the job he currently holds.

"I thought I'd come down here to Mexico to complete the process of my conversion," he told me. "I have a deep connection to the South—I'm a small town boy—and I figured on going back to pastor a church in a small town in South Carolina. But here's what I found out: the conversion never stops. The minute I start to feel comfortable, the reality down here confronts me again and I'm converted again. Nowadays I've come to expect conversion to happen. I look forward to it."

Mark dropped me off at the Migrant Resource Center, which occupies a space that appears to have been a shoe store once or some other small-scale retail operation. It's located just beyond the Mexican checkpoint at the border and directly behind the Mexican customs inspection area. It's a perfect location to help those who have been deported.

Started in 2005 as a joint effort of *Frontera de Cristo* and the Sagrada Familia Roman Catholic Church in Agua Prieta, the Migrant Resource Center grew out of an idea that came to Mark Adams's mind in the dead of winter as he was handing out blankets to migrants deported by the Border Patrol with nowhere to go and nothing to keep them warm. By the summer of 2009, the Migrant Resource Center had helped more than forty thousand individuals, operating on the dedication of volunteers, a lot of prayer, and a budget of twelve thousand dollars a year. That goes further in Mexico using pesos than it would in the United States using dollars, but it's a paltry sum in any currency. By contrast, the Douglas, Arizona Border Patrol station's budget, according to Mark Adams, is around eight million dollars annually.

When I arrived at the center, it was quiet. Beto Ramos, the center's Mexican coordinator (all *Frontera de Cristo* projects have both Mexican and American coordinators), greeted me and showed me around. Beto is a thirty-something Catholic layman with kind eyes behind Sarah Palin glasses. Three Roman Catholic seminarians sat around a rickety aluminum desk, surfing the Internet together on a laptop. Shelves in the back of the center held first aid supplies and used clothes. Bologna sandwiches and burritos sat in a refrigerator. A fresh pot of coffee and a water cooler were standing by, ready to dispense warmth and hydration. Posters encouraging migrants to think twice before trying to cross the border again and advising them of their rights covered the walls; between the posters were notices from families looking for loved ones who had disappeared into the desert.

The migrant center meets a set of basic but important needs. After being apprehended by the Border Patrol and spending time in detention, migrants without too many prior entries and without criminal records have the option of signing a voluntary deportation document. If they sign the document, the Border Patrol takes them to the border, usually after they have spent several hours in detention. When they come across they have few or no possessions. They have no place to stay and nowhere in particular to go. Often they are hungry and thirsty. Sometimes they are hurt or ill. Their shoes are always unlaced. (The Border Patrol confiscates shoelaces to prevent suicide by hanging and to make it difficult for escapees to run; the laces are eventually given back, but their owners are not given time to relace their shoes before they are sent across the border into Mexico.) "That's how you will know them," Beto warned me. "They'll come in here holding their shoelaces."

When migrants come into the center they receive food and water, and volunteers administer first aid as needed. If the recently deported need a change of clothes, they are offered a chance to peruse the used clothing in the back of the center. Beto and his volunteers find beds for the returnees in various shelters around Agua Prieta. The clients may use the center's phones to call home and they may purchase deeply discounted bus tickets home into the interior of Mexico.

The Migrant Resource Center keeps copious and detailed notes on everyone helped. I looked at the notes for earlier in the day and discovered that before I got there, the center had helped fifty-two returning migrants. Those returning had stayed in detention between three and twelve hours. While in detention, most ate only crackers and drank water from a hose. One group of the returnees reported being given neither food nor water. Many of the returnees said they were subjected to racist and demeaning language while in detention. One woman reported being sexually assaulted—groped by a Border Patrol agent after he forced her to remove her shirt.

"We asked the Border Patrol about this kind of thing," Mark Adams told me the next day, over a lunch of *caldo de queso*, a cheese soup that is popular among locals. "I inquired about the Border Patrol treatment of migrants. They denied any wrongdoing, but they did admit that they get no human rights training. None. But they get training in marksmanship once a month."

The Migrant Resource Center's records of abuse and neglect experienced by migrants at the hands of the Border Patrol confirm the findings of an analysis of confidential studies of Immigration and Customs Enforcement detention centers by the United Nations High Commissioner for Refugees and the American Bar Association. The American Civil Liberties Union of Southern California published the finding in 2009. At the conclusion of the one hundred-and-seventy-page report the authors write,

> There is no question that the nation's immigrant detention system is broken to its core. The findings in this report as well as those recently documented by various government and independent agencies reveal pervasive and extreme violations of the government's own detention standards as well as fundamental violations of basic human rights and notions of dignity.[4]

My orientation to the work of the center ended when a young Honduran man named Hernán came in with a bag of *pupusas*. *Pupusas* are a Central American dish made of corn meal surrounding a combination of cheese and meat. They look like thick tortillas, act like stuffed pita, and taste wonderful. Hernán asked me if I'd ever eaten a *pupusa*. He seemed like the kind of person who likes introducing strangers to new experiences. "Yes," I told him, feeling a little bad about disappointing him, "We have some really good Salvadoran restaurants in the neighborhood where I live."

Hernán smiled a lot, and his laugh was infectious, but his good cheer disappeared when I mentioned "*pupusa*" and "El Salvador" in the same sentence. "*Pupusas* are from Honduras!" His demeanor grew intense and angry. "El Salvador always gets the credit. *We* taught *them* how to make *pupusas*!" I was reminded of how arguments between Jews and Palestinians about the origins of falafel have led to the further destabilization of peace in the Holy Land. Who knows? Maybe food served in pocket bread inspires conflict no matter who eats it.

After I agreed that Honduran *pupusas* are far superior to those served up by Salvadoran posers, the smile returned to Hernán's face. He told us about his journey north and his desire to enter the United States. He rode a freight train north from Central America, and when he reached Agua Prieta his leg got caught in the coupling mechanism between two cars. He spent a long time in the hospital and now makes a living by selling *pupusas*. "Maybe next February, I'll go north," he told us. "My leg is better, and I'm pure Inca. We're a strong and resourceful people."

"Inca?" we asked. What the seminarians and I had learned about the pre-Columbian history of the Americas did not include a knowledge that Incas lived in Central America.

"Oh yes," he told us, "we were going to take over the world before the Spanish beat us to it."

Maybe so, and anyway, no one in the room was about to question the ethnic heritage of a man who got so passionate about the national origin of *pupusas*.

All at once, while we were thinking about *pupusas* and the territorial expansion of the Incan Empire, the little room was full of tired, wilted, hungry, and thirsty men, who, just minutes before, had been in U.S. custody. They smelled of dust and sweat. None of their shoes had shoelaces. They had the empty stare of those who had just endured intense hardship. Beto and the seminarians sprang to life like firefighters responding to an alarm.

We found chairs for the recently repatriated, ten men who looked to be between the ages of eighteen and sixty. They seemed to come from a wide variety of backgrounds—some wore stylish and expensive-looking clothes, while others looked like *campesinos*, peasants from the countryside. One man had a mustache that looked like it had been ripped from an old photo of the great Mexican revolutionary Emiliano Zapata, only instead of sporting an oversized, straw sombrero and bandoliers, this man was wearing a Denver Nuggets jersey over baggy denim shorts.

We gave them water, coffee, and bologna sandwiches. They were ravenous and parched, though they were luckier than most returnees who visit the center. During twelve hours of detention they had each eaten a single burrito. Beto interviewed the men, asking them about their experiences in detention and advising them about options for the immediate future: free lodging for a few days, the possibility of buying a bus ticket home at a deep discount.

Most of the men accepted the offer of a bed. Two decided to return home. Emiliano Zapata of the Denver Nuggets walked out into the night, his shoes relaced and a change of clothes from the center's supply of second-hand garments hanging in a plastic bag at his side. I last saw him silhouetted against the lights of the Mexican customs inspection facility at the border crossing as he walked out into the sleeping streets of Agua Prieta. Perhaps he would find the hope and determination necessary to attempt the crossing again, and perhaps he would make it this time. Or perhaps he would get caught and deported again, and he would return to the center once more on another night just like this. With life along the border it's hard to say.

"Immigration Affects All of Us": Life in a Border Town

I'd had a bit of a journey getting to the Migrant Resource Center. When I arrived in Douglas a few hours before the start of the prayer vigil, Mark Adams had sent me across the border in an old, wheezy twelve-seater Chevy van named "The Fitz." Evidently, the van, which belonged to an orphanage friendly with, but not connected to, *Frontera de Cristo*, was donated by a man whose last name was either Fitzpatrick or Fitzhugh or Fitzgerald—no one remembered exactly. I headed south with the harmony of V8 on bass, old fan belts on soprano, and the A/C fan somewhere in between; four wheels badly in need of alignment provided a rhythm section.

My assignment was to meet a young man named Jordan Bullard at the Migrant Resource Center where, later that evening, I would eat *pupusas* with a man who fancied himself an Inca, and feed bologna sandwiches to men sent across the border without shoelaces. It seemed an easy enough thing to do—Mark had given me great directions—but I didn't find the place right away, and I discovered with a note of concern that every time I drove into a blind alley and had to put The Fitz into reverse so that I could back up and try my luck down another back street or side road, the engine died, and each time it did, I became, for a moment, a man of passionate prayer. I invoked the name of Jesus, his mother, and Santo Toribio Romo, just in case the narrow petitions of a Protestant weren't enough to turn over a Detroit engine made during the Carter administration. I simply wasn't sure what one did with a broken-down, half-turned-around, twelve-seater Chevy van in Mexico. Finally, I parked The Fitz with its front end a foot from the rusted, solid steel wall that announces the international border in that part of Agua Prieta, and I set off to look for the migrant center on foot. I asked a policeman for directions, and, looking at me as if I were daft, he pointed to the building directly in front of us. Just another lost *gringo* wandering in the new reality that begins when you cross the border.

The building I'd failed to see was painted day-glo lemon and lime. On the wall, painted freehand, were the words,

> *CENTRO DE RECOURSOS DE MIGRANTES*
> *Servicos:*
> *Agua y comida,*
> *Orientación,*
> *Apoyo Médico,*
> *Y Más*
> *Servicios Gratuitos Para Deportados*
> *Exclusivamente.*

(MIGRANT RESOURCE CENTER
Services:
Water and food,
Orientation,
Medical Support,
And More
Free Services For the Deported,
Exclusively.)

Jordan Bullard, Beto's American counterpart at the center, is a handsome young man with a firm handshake and a full head of lively, unmanaged hair. Like Mark Adams, he is from South Carolina, and he smiles as he speaks with a slow drawl. He wears his sunglasses upside down and pushed up on his head. I came to learn that Jordan plays the guitar and rides a well-aged mountain bike back and forth across the border and through the streets of Agua Prieta wearing flip-flops.

Jordan put his bike in The Fitz, and I, having lost confidence in my ability to find my way around Agua Prieta, just yards south of the international border, handed over the keys. Wanting to be helpful, I warned him that the van seemed to be allergic to the suggestion that it go backward. Jordan looked at me benevolently and switched off the air conditioner. "Doesn't work anyway." He pointed out. "Now she'll back up just fine." And she did. Jordan pulled The Fitz into Agua Prieta traffic and we were off to a community center run by *Frontera de Cristo* on the outskirts of town.

I asked Jordan what drew him to the border. "I came down here three years ago and was really impressed with what everyone was doing," he said as he expertly nosed The Fitz in and out of traffic and through the city. "It was a time in my life when I thought that helping people was something I really should be doing.

"This is a place that has a lot of need and it's also a place that is controversial, just because of the nature of American politics and American people. I see this as a form of racism, where instead of African Americans bearing the brunt of the racism in the United States, I see Hispanic people bearing the brunt of the racism in the United States. In a lot of ways it's a lot more subtle to me and in some ways its not very subtle at all, and in many ways it is frightening because it's so militarized here and people think that just because it's the border they can get away with prejudice and racism."

When we arrived at the *Frontera de Cristo* community center, we met Angel and Maria Elena Valencia, who are colleagues of Mark Adams's at *Frontera de Cristo*. The community center was bustling with life. A daily vacation Bible school was in full swing. Lunch preparations were making the place smell good, and a pickup combo made up of ten-year-old girls on guitar, bass, and drums was playing praise songs. Jordan found an unused guitar and joined the band. I sat down with Angel and Maria Elena, then asked them how the United States' increased enforcement along the border had affected the community in which they lived and worked.

"Migration is something that touches every part of life in Agua Prieta." Angel told me. "Everyone knows someone—a friend or a family member—who has crossed the border or who has been caught trying. Immigration affects all of us."

Maria Elena is a motherly woman with a nurturing countenance.

> It's important when you're talking about migration to see the human side of the people who immigrate because they carry with them feelings, hope, illusions. People have to put a lot into play. They have to sell belongings, land, and businesses to reach the other side. If they don't make it, they return and now they have nothing. Many times they even lose their families because now they have nothing.
>
> What's worse is that those who help the people cross—the *coyotes*—have no pity. They don't see the migrants as people, they see them as merchandise, not as human beings, but as people who will give them money. It's a business for them. It doesn't matter to them what is the dream or motive or reason for crossing. They only see money. And if there's no money the people get left behind.
>
> Those who end up in Agua Prieta and cannot afford to cross don't know what to do or how to react, because what are they going to do? Go home where they have nothing, or stay here? Often these are people without the moral or mental resources or the strength to get back up and return to life.
>
> It's important to take into account not just the political or the economic issues involved with immigration, but also the feelings of the people.

Beyond Fair Trade: Working for Justice, Cup by Cup

Jordan and I left Angel, Maria Elena, and the vacation Bible school kids at the community center. We climbed back into The Fitz and went to get a cup of coffee at the roasting operation of *Café Justo*, Just Coffee, an economic development project run by *Frontera de Cristo*.

Café Justo is an economic development project that arose out of a conviction that undocumented migration across the U.S./Mexico border, with all of its dangers and social difficulties, will continue unabated unless economic conditions change in Mexico. No amount of fencing or high tech gadgetry and no increase of Border Patrol personnel is going to stem the tide. The café's founders feel that such measures only force migrants out into the desert to make an increasingly dangerous journey. Certainly, no amount of moralizing or preaching can keep people from going north to find jobs.

After arriving in Douglas/Agua Prieta in 1998, it didn't take long for Mark Adams to figure out that real and sustained economic development in Mexico was the only way to keep people from risking their lives by crossing the border in the desert. As he became acquainted with life on the border south of Tucson, Mark found that the population of Agua Prieta had an extraordinarily large community of former coffee farmers from Chiapas, Mexico's southernmost state. These were people who had been forced off their land after a global drop in the price of coffee. Most of the former coffee farmers from Chiapas were looking for work in the manufacturing plants, or *maquiladoras*, that sprang up along the border after the passage of NAFTA; many hoped to cross the border illegally to find work in the United States. Work in a *maquiladora* pays twice or three times what can be earned by a coffee grower in Chiapas, and a job doing unskilled labor in the United States might pull in twice the paycheck earned by a *maquiladora* employee.

Because the Presbyterian Church is particularly strong in the south of Mexico, many of the former coffee growers from Chiapas were Presbyterians who worshiped with the Presbyterian community in Agua Prieta. Within that community discussions began around what could be done to change the economic conditions in the coffee-growing regions of Mexico so that northward immigration would not be a financial necessity.

The economics of coffee are tricky. For many years coffee was a stable cash crop, and before the late 1980s few people left the coffee farms of Chiapas in favor of opportunity in the north. When the price of coffee beans dropped in the late 1980s and early 1990s, however, farmers left their land in record numbers. The depression in the value of coffee came at a great price to coffee-growing communities in Chiapas. Families were separated. Labor became scarce.

What's weird is that while the price of beans tanked, the retail price of coffee actually rose. Customers in the United States and Europe saw the price of coffee skyrocket with the proliferation of Starbucks and other high-end coffee houses around the world, but none of the economic benefits of the growing coffee industry filtered down to Chiapas.

Many organizations have attempted to address the economic inequality inherent in the coffee industry by engaging in fair trade. Fair trade organizations and businesses often roast beans that are purchased directly from the growers, thereby eliminating the middlemen, and passing the distribution profits to the growers.

Fair trade is a good model, but the Presbyterian coffee growers from Chiapas wanted more. They recognized that the biggest profit in the coffee economic chain is earned by those who roast coffee and sell it to consumers, so together with Mark Adams and Tommy Bassett (about whom we'll learn more later) the coffee growers in Agua Prieta began to dream about a coffee collective through which farmers in Chiapas could sell a finished product directly to consumers in the United States. *Café Justo* was born out of these dreams.

With an infusion of microcredit cash, *Café Justo* purchased an industrial roaster. A trip to the impoverished village of Salvador Urbina, Chiapas, to speak with relatives of the former coffee growers now living in Agua Prieta identified farmers willing to participate in a coffee growing and roasting collective in which coffee grown near Mexico's Guatemalan border would be roasted, packaged, and marketed on Mexico's American border. The farmers in Salvador Urbina are paid a fair price for their coffee, workers in Agua Prieta are paid a living wage, and all of the profits are invested in the communities where the coffee is grown.

Most of the coffee produced by *Café Justo* sells to churches in the United States. It's a niche market, but profits have made a profound impact in Chiapas. In the years since *Café Justo* was founded in 2002, the village of Salvador Urbina has changed dramatically. Before *Café Justo*, the town's population was eight thousand and falling. Now, more than ten thousand souls call Salvador Urbina home. Thanks to the profits of *Café Justo*, local folks have been able to renovate schools, open businesses, and connect Salvador Urbina to the Internet. Today, few people leave Salvador Urbina with dreams of crossing the U.S./Mexican border illegally. By 2008, the *Café Justo* cooperative had expanded to include farmers in El Aguila, Chiapas, and Totonaco, Vera Cruz; a second roasting operation opened in Tijuana, Baja California. Conversations have begun with coffee growers in Haiti. *Café Justo* is going multinational.[5]

As we left *Café Justo* and headed back across the border in The Fitz, Jordan told me what Mark Adams also had told me: that if I wanted a good perspective on immigration and the border, I should talk to Tommy Bassett, who, together with Mark Adams and the coffee farmers from Chiapas, was responsible for the success of *Café Justo*.

Tommy works as a developer at *Frontera de Cristo*'s Just Trade Center, which seeks to expand the vision of *Café Justo* by starting other coffee cooperatives or other product cooperatives based on the model of *Café Justo*. The Just Trade Center does training for those seeking to start fair-trade businesses, provides assistance with legal matters, and strategizes marketing. Sometimes they are able to extend microcredit to cooperatives in need of capital.

It's work that Tommy enjoys. His is a meaningful occupation that keeps him close to the border, a place he loves. A native of Minnesota, Tommy first moved to Douglas, Arizona to manage a *maquiladora* in Agua Prieta. We sat down together in the Douglas, Arizona offices of *Frontera de Cristo* over full mugs of coffee from *Café Justo*. I asked Tommy how he got involved with issues of migration.

> I got immediately introduced to migration coming down here. For me, it was with turnover rates in the factory because the turnover rate was about two-and-a-half percent per week on average. That means 100 percent a year, and as the factory grows that means that a lot of resources in the factory get devoted to training.

Tommy's factory grew. At one point it was, with 4,500 employees, the largest employer in the Mexican State of Sonora. Eventually, Taiwanese buyers purchased the company that owned Tommy's *maquiladora*, and the manufacturing operations moved to Asia.

When his job moved, Tommy knew he couldn't leave the border. It had become his home. "When I'm not here on the border I really miss it. There's a certain tension here—not all bad tension—and also the interplay of two cultures and two languages. It's really cool." After his *maquiladora*'s manufacturing operations moved to Asia, Tommy made a living with his camera and as a writer, becoming an activist around immigration issues.

Douglas, Arizona is a small town, and the community of those interested in issues of immigration is even smaller. Eventually, Tommy met Mark Adams in nearby Bisbee, "at a Hanukkah party thrown by a Jewish atheist to protest Christmas." Tommy laughed. "We started talking about coffee. I've been through the whole coffee process from drinking instant coffee to Folgers to getting into whole beans, to flavored coffee, to really high quality. I love drinking coffee." Tommy followed his love of coffee into employment with *Frontera de Cristo* through the development of *Café Justo* and the Just Trade Center.

Tommy is a corpulent man with a full beard. His long hair is pulled back into a French braid. He looks like a combination of Grizzly Adams and Captain Haddock, with a hint of San Francisco's Haight-Ashbury thrown in for flavor. His blue eyes are intense, and he laughs a lot. I asked Tommy how things had changed along the border during the twenty years he has called Douglas, Arizona and Agua Prieta, Sonora home. "This part of the border is kind of like Savannah, Georgia," he told me. "It's a place that has kind of prided itself on hospitality and taking time enough to talk."

Tommy took a pensive swig of coffee.

> There's this community that has a fence that goes through it. The fence didn't work very well until a few years before 9/11. Children who were going to school in Douglas would just run across the border if they lived in eastern Agua Prieta because it was just too far to go all the way west to the port of entry and then all the way back to school. People flowed back and forth in a natural ebb

and tide with respect to agriculture work, seasons, and cycles as well as just normal holiday stuff. But as militarization increased, now you had to have a passport to get over the border and it's a big federal offense if you give someone a ride and don't reasonably validate their citizenship. People get arrested for putting water in the desert up in Tucson, and down here people won't go into Mexico because maybe they have a parking ticket from ten years ago that they didn't pay for, or maybe they have a relative that is undocumented and is living in the United States and another relative who's trying to get legal documentation. So there's a bunch of fear.

And the nature of the community has changed. The Border Patrol is the biggest employer here. We have the biggest Border Patrol station—I think in the world but certainly along the U.S./Mexico border. These guys start out at around fifty thousand dollars a year—maybe forty-seven or forty-eight—and there's five hundred of them plus the administrative people, and that completely changes the nature of the community. Of course, the political people around here don't say anything because the Border Patrol people stay at the local hotels, eat at the local restaurants, and the people who get harassed don't have any options. They're poor and disenfranchised.

As the militarization of the [U.S.] border increased, it made crossing the border more difficult. Of course it is much more difficult for people crossing in the desert, but it also is hard for people with passports. There is a lot more fear that came into both communities—Agua Prieta and Douglas. Now all of a sudden there are people with automatic weapons driving around the streets, and helicopters and drones, horse patrols and motorcycle patrols, and unmarked cars.

Watching all this has been really challenging, especially in a place that has a strong Hispanic influence where family and friendship is something bigger than you'd see in a lot of Midwestern towns like where I grew up. To see all this militarization and fear coming to the border has been bad. It's sobering how quickly it can change.

We finished the coffee in our mugs. It was time to head to the McDonald's parking lot along the border to participate in the vigil described at the beginning of this chapter. Not knowing that Tommy was one of the chief organizers of the vigil, I asked him if he would be taking part. He told me that his emotional and spiritual health depended upon it.

> We've been working on border issues for a while and without the prayer vigil we'd be too depressed because any way you measure it, things have just gotten worse and worse. Our nation's immigration policies are an abject failure. More people are in the United States than ever before. More people are dying crossing the borders. Without the vigil it would be pretty depressing.
>
> Even though we're praying for the people who are dying and who have died and who are in the desert, it's a time for community and for getting centered. I know there are people who are really involved in migration issues who are stated agnostics or atheists or who come from no faith tradition. They seem to do just fine, but I couldn't. The vigil is a source of strength.

Twenty minutes later we met up again at the McDonald's parking lot, where we prayed together, remembered the names of the dead, and found strength.

The next day I met up with Angel Valencia at the Migrant Resource Center. He and I were going together into the desert to leave water for migrants, which I'll talk about in the next chapter. While I waited for him, I spoke with two middle-aged women who had just been deported. They bore the scratches of mesquite thorns on every bit of exposed skin. Their eyes were bloodshot. One woman's face was beaten and swollen, her eye blackened like that of a losing pugilist. She told me she had fallen down a ravine somewhere out in the wilderness south of Tucson. The sisters were eating instant soup provided by Jordan Bullard, who was on duty at the center that morning.

Both women lived in Los Angeles, but they had returned to Mexico to attend the funeral of an older sister. Both had American-born teenaged children living in Los Angeles, and both told me they would set out again, later that day, to cross the border once more, because children need their mothers, especially when they're teenagers and require a watchful eye. Besides, now that their oldest sister had died there was no family left in Mexico. Heading north was their only choice.

Angel found me talking with the sisters, and, before bidding them goodbye, he and I promised to keep the sisters' journey in our prayers. As we left the Migrant Resource Center I kept my promise, silently asking God to give the two women traveling mercies and to keep their names off the white crosses that line the last few blocks of a border town street from McDonald's to Mexico every Tuesday.

Chapter 8

Water in the Desert

Waters shall break forth in the wilderness,
and streams in the desert;
the burning sand shall become a pool,
and the thirsty ground springs of water;
the haunt of jackals shall become a swamp,
the grass shall become reeds and rushes.
A highway shall be there,
and it shall be called the Holy Way.

—*Isaiah 35:6b–8a*

For years I have harbored a stereotype of those who go out into the desert to leave water for migrants crossing into the United States from Mexico on foot: they are white and progressive. Often religious, they worship at Quaker meetings, Unitarian Universalist congregations, and liberal, mainline Protestant churches. They shop at farmers' markets, and, if they can afford them, drive hybrid automobiles on which they may have bumper stickers that declare a commitment to peace, support for a local public radio station (extra points if it's Pacifica instead of NPR), an affirmation that "hate is not a family value," and a desire to keep Berkeley (or Austin or Bisbee, Arizona) weird.

In short, they're people like me, and I met a few such folks, volunteers with an organization called No More Deaths, while I was in Douglas, Arizona/Agua Prieta, Sonora; but when I went out into the desert to leave water for thirsty wayfarers, I went with Leonardo, a recovering alcoholic and cocaine addict participating in a rehab program in Agua Prieta called CRREDA.[1]

CRREDA's approach to getting on and staying on the wagon is creative. The folks in recovery live in a compound that also serves as a home for people with mental illness. While enduring detox and working the twelve steps, those living at CRREDA take care of their mentally ill roommates. They wash, dress, and feed those who are unable to help themselves. "They are a blessing. We learn to honor them and love them," Leonardo told me. "They are my friends now."

As a part of its program, CRREDA also requires those seeking treatment to engage in community service, once they are far enough along in recovery that they are able to go outside the compound. Leaving water in the desert for migrants is one of CRREDA's most important projects. In the last few years CRREDA volunteers have left more than 100,000 gallons of water in a series of blue fifty-five gallon drums placed under black walnut trees along paths used by migrants on their way to the border.

It is work that Leonardo loves. "It reminds me that I have a meaningful life, that I can still do something important for others, even though I've lost so much to drugs and alcohol," he said.

Leonardo's English is perfect. "I'm from Oregon," he explained to me when I started talking to him in Spanish. "I lived there for thirty years." Judging by his looks, thirty years in Oregon wasn't going to leave a lot of time for living anywhere else. "We moved there when I was two," he told me. "I am a mechanic and a union carpenter. I was married and I have three kids."

After a series of drug- and alcohol-related arrests and a failure to appear in court, the court gave Leonardo a deportation order and he ended up in a place he hardly knew where they spoke a language he barely understood, but it saved his life. "My mom found this place for me online," Leonardo explained. "I tried a rehab program in Oregon, but they were too easy on me. Then I tried another place here in Mexico, but it didn't work. CRREDA is good because we work with our mentally ill friends, and we do stuff like this," he said, in reference to our trip into the desert. "I like it here."

Five of us—Leonardo and I; Angel Valencia from *Frontera de Cristo*; his daughter, Claudia, who is a flautist from Chihuahua; and another CRREDA resident named Carlos—climbed into an old pickup truck that looked more like automotive salvage than transportation. Claudia and I rode up front with Leonardo; Angel and Carlos rode in the bed with a spare tire, a hose, and a two-hundred-gallon tank full of drinking water.

The truck lurched, rattled, and wheezed through the occasionally paved streets of Agua Prieta and onto a two-lane highway. Leonardo had to turn the wheel about forty-five degrees before the steering mechanism moved the truck appreciably one way or another; I soon figured out that the box my right foot kept instinctively trying to use as a brake actually was an open-faced subwoofer. Claudia was white-knuckling a straw hat decorated with silk roses that she had brought for protection from the sun.

Ten miles out of Agua Prieta, Leonardo guided us off the road and into a barnyard belonging to a friendly rancher whose son had once lived at CRREDA. A streak of lightning flashed across the western horizon and I realized that I might have more things to worry about than not wearing a seatbelt on a Mexican highway in a pickup that might have been rejected as insufficiently drivable by the Joad family in *The Grapes of Wrath*. By wandering out into the Sonora desert in a thunderstorm during the monsoon season, I was going into a place prone to flash flooding, to visit, among other things, a border fence that is made of iron and stretches for hundreds of miles in each direction. For years I had known that the border fence was a lightning rod, but until that moment I had assumed that designation was only a metaphor.

Thunder rolled. "The angels are bowling," said Leonardo, flashing a devious smile, and we were off into the desert with a hop and a whine and a cloud of exhaust-infused dust.

Border Crossings

It is impossible to know exactly how many people cross the U.S./Mexico border through the desert each year. The United States Department of Homeland Security reports that the United States Border Patrol apprehended more than seven hundred thousand people crossing the southwest border in 2008, and that the number of apprehensions has been declining since 2005.[2] These numbers are, however, somewhat misleading, because they represent events and not individuals. Many people attempt to cross the border and are caught several times before entering the United States successfully or giving up and returning home. And no one can count the number of people who cross the desert border without getting caught.

Nor can the number of those who die trying to cross the desert border be known with anything approaching accuracy. The United States Government Accountability Office, using information provided by the Border Patrol, estimated that 2,179 people perished along the border between 1995 and 2005.[3] Sources in Arizona calculate that between January 1, 2004 and December 31, 2009, an average of 223 people were found dead each year along the border in Arizona alone, putting that single-state stretch of desert on a course to have as many fatalities in a decade as were reported on the entire border in the decade before. Many of the deaths in Arizona occurred right across the border from the area where we were headed in Leonardo's bucket of bolts.[4]

After leaving the highway, we followed ranch roads into the desert, where green mesquite and ocotillo set their roots into red clay and sand. After fifteen minutes on the ranch road we left through a rusty gate and Leonardo drove, as if by instinct, into the mesquite. He seemed to know where he was going. For Claudia's sake we tried to keep our conversation in Spanish, but English kept slipping back in. "We're probably being watched," he told me. Out here the *narcos* keep a close eye on who might be moving into their territory." *Narcos*. Drug smugglers. Now I had another thing to worry about. The drug cartels in northern Mexico are notoriously violent and cruel. "Actually, they leave us alone," he told me. "They know we're doing good work. The Mexican Army, too. They're out here a lot looking for the *narcos*, but I think they're glad we're helping Mexican citizens. It's not like on the other side where the Border Patrol doesn't like people leaving water. *Las Patrollas*—the Patrols—are probably watching us too, but we're in Mexico. They cannot do anything about our water." There was a thought: in Leonardo's mind and—no doubt in the minds of others—the *narcos* have a better reputation than does the Border Patrol. It's a different world south of the border.

For one thing, leaving water in the desert for migrants is legal south of the border. Not so in the United States: six weeks before Leonardo took me out into the desert, Walt Staton, a twenty-seven-year-old volunteer with No More Deaths, received a guilty verdict for criminal littering after the U.S. Border Patrol caught him leaving jugs of water in the Buenos Aires National Wildlife Refuge, south of Tucson, an area favored by those crossing the border. The assistant U.S. attorney working on the case asked the judge to give Staton the harshest possible punishment—five years of probation and a five thousand dollar fine.

In the minds of prosecutors, Staton's case was not just about protecting mule deer and the endangered masked bobwhite quail from the very real dangers of plastic litter. Noting that No More Deaths volunteers often write *buena suerte* ("good luck") on the bottles, Lawrence Lee, the assistant U.S. attorney for the district of Tucson, in a memo to the court, wrote, "The obvious conclusion is that the defendant and No More Deaths wish to aid illegal aliens in their entry attempt. His actions are not about humanitarian efforts, but about protesting the immigration policies of the United States."

Later that summer, Staton received a light sentence—three hundred hours of community service picking up trash, a year's probation, and a court order to stay out of the Buenos Aires National Wildlife Refuge.[5]

It's hard to know how serious a crime it is to leave water in the parts of the desert ceded to the United States by the Treaty of Guadalupe and the Gadsden Purchase.[6] When he was found guilty of littering, Walter Staton was one of perhaps a dozen people charged with similar offenses while leaving water for migrants; I soon realized that it could happen to anyone—even to me, had I been dispensing water north of the border. Two days after I was in the desert I was in the company of several assistant U.S. attorneys. It was a congenial and social gathering. When I mentioned my trip to the desert with Leonardo I got a few raised eyebrows. "Aiding and abetting," one of the prosecutors said slowly, looking at me through eyelids at half-mast. It was a good-natured jibe, and we were being friendly, but still, it was a comfort to point out that I had been in Sonora at the time, and if there was a problem with my humanitarian gestures, the case would have to be made in a Mexican courtroom, where Leonardo assured me there would be no trouble.

It certainly didn't feel like a criminal's errand, as grinding and bouncing, we made our way through the desert topography of sandpits and dry creek beds until we came to an arroyo, a wash used as a trail by northward-bound migrants. Carlos hopped off the back of the truck to make sure the track down into the arroyo would still accommodate the water truck. "It changes all the time, especially during the rainy season," Leonardo explained as we dropped down onto the arroyo's sandy bottom.

The wheels spun until the truck rested on its rear differential. We were stuck.

"Sunnuva bitch!" Leonardo looked at me. Then he remembered he was sharing the truck's cab with a preacher who happened to speak English, and the daughter of a preacher who probably spoke *that* much English.

"Oops." He smiled apologetically, but he needn't have worried, since I was of a similar mind. I really didn't want to be stuck in a desert wash during flash flood season. I had visions of the truck being washed down the arroyo by some torrential rush of water.

We jumped out of the truck. We pushed. We put rocks under the tires. Leonardo sent rooster tails of sand into the air as the tires spun and, somehow, perhaps by the intercession of Santo Toribio Romo, the wheels became dislodged and we hopped back in and pulled up out of the arroyo at the first watering station. Two blue, plastic, fifty-five gallon drums sat on a wooden frame. A fire pit was nearby, and the evidence of humans was scattered all around—discarded tuna fish cans, empty water and soda-pop bottles. Someone had hung a roll of toilet paper on a bush. A blue flag—now a recognizable landmark for water on both sides of the border—marked the site.

"I'm glad we do this," said Leonardo, as the hose filled up the water drums. "It ain't right that people should die out here just because they have a job on the other side of the border."

We decided driving the truck further down the arroyo was too big a risk, so we left the task of filling the other water barrels for another day, but we continued down the arroyo on foot, to check the water level at another drinking station, and to visit the border fence.

"I saw a javelina out here once," Leonardo reported. Javelinas are pig-like animals that live in the Sonora Desert. "And look," he said. "There are pumas out here." Leonardo was pointing at a paw print in the sand. I didn't see any wild mammals in the desert, but I did see a dung beetle pushing a ball of the substance for which it was named. The ball was about four times the size of the bug and the bug was pushing the ball with its back legs as it walked on its front legs, in reverse. My eight-year-old inner child was thrilled.

While I was looking at the arroyo's sandy bottom for bugs and paw prints I saw my first pair of discarded pants. I pulled them out of the sand and held them up for Leonardo.

"Yea, we find those a lot," he told me. "We like to go through the pockets to see if we can find any identification. When we find someone's I.D. we turn it in to the police, in case that person is missing and a loved one is looking for him. Usually people just change their pants and leave the old ones. They don't want to carry too much clothes. But sometimes not. You never know." We only ever found sand in the pockets of the pants half buried on the arroyo floor but we looked anyway, wondering if the buzzards circling over the mesquite in the distance were looking down on the person whose legs once filled these rotting garments with life. We moved on, under a railroad track that runs parallel to the border, and northward to the great iron fence itself, an enormous line of rusting steel that runs as far as the eye can see in either direction.

Fences and Neighbors

The border between the United States and Mexico stretches for two thousand miles between the Gulf of Mexico and the Pacific Ocean. It follows the Rio Grande (or *Rio Bravo*, if you live in Mexico) between Brownsville, Texas, on the Gulf Coast and El Paso, Texas, where the river makes a bend northward into the mountains of New Mexico. Between El Paso, Texas and San Ysidro, California, just south of San Diego, the border runs through the Chihuahua and Sonora deserts, and over high and desolate mountainous terrain. It is a harsh and unforgiving geography.

It's hard to imagine why a nation already blessed with the protection afforded by a border of largely uninhabited deserts and mountains and a wide river also needs a fence along its southern flank, but for reasons that are political more than they are practical, the system of fences and barriers demarcating the border is growing.

For most of the years since the establishment of the current U.S./Mexico border by the Treaty of Guadalupe Hidalgo and the Gadsden Purchase the border has had little in the way of demarcation. Near larger cities and busier ports of entry there were fences made of chain link or barbed wire, but the border was generally open to those who wanted to walk across it.

In 1993, the situation began to change. In an effort to stem the tide of smugglers crossing the border at the beach in San Ysidro, California, the United States government erected a solid steel fence made of surplus Viet Nam-era landing mats—large rectangles of grooved steel designed for use in the construction of temporary runways. In one of the stranger engineering oversights one encounters along the border, whoever installed the steel sections of fence did so in such a way that the grooves run horizontally, providing a perfect ladder for those desiring to climb over the fence. But never mind. The fence ran fourteen miles inland from the beach.

By 1995, with the initiation of "Operation Gatekeeper," a strategic, multifaceted anti-immigration program along the San Diego-area border, the Border Patrol extended the steel fence out to the mountains east of San Diego and the building of walls along the U.S./Mexico border has never really abated since. In 2006 President George W. Bush signed the "Secure Fence Act of 2006," which authorized the building of 700 miles of fencing along the border. "Ours is a nation of immigrants," the president said while signing the act, "We're also a nation of law. Unfortunately, the United States has not been in complete control of its borders for decades and, therefore, illegal immigration has been on the rise. We have a responsibility to address these challenges. We have a responsibility to enforce our laws. We have a responsibility to secure our borders. We take this responsibility seriously."[7] By the summer of 2009, the southern borders of California, Arizona, and New Mexico were almost entirely fenced off.[8]

Our path up the arroyo ended at the border fence, but the arroyo didn't stop there, nor did the water that runs down the wash during the seasonal floods. "The fence keeps getting washed out here. They can't keep it fixed." Leonardo pointed through the fence at the detritus of several attempts to stop the flow of water down the arroyo and across the border. There were steel grates and cement pilings littering the arroyo on the American side. "And check this out." Leonardo grabbed a section of the fence whose footings were buried in the arroyo sand. He rocked it back and forth; ten feet above his head the fence moved three feet in either direction. "This section is going to go with the next serious flood." Some words of Robert Frost's poem "Mending Wall" came to my mind:

> Something there is that doesn't love a wall,
> That sends the frozen-ground-swell under it,
> And spills the upper boulders in the sun,
> And makes gaps even two can pass abreast.

Lightning flashed, thunder rolled and the air increasingly was thick with the smell of rain. It was time to leave the desert. We walked back up the arroyo, the threat of flash floods notwithstanding, because the mesquite was too thick in that part of the desert, and mesquite thorns are nasty. I have no doubt that if mesquite grew in Palestine, someone in the Roman cohort would have used it to fashion Jesus' crown of thorns.

We climbed out of the arroyo at the watering station where we had left the car, leaving it to Leonardo to maneuver his beast back up onto the desert floor, and as the truck shrieked and popped back to life the rain started to fall. It wasn't a gentle rain either. Each drop contained maybe a tablespoon of water and it fell as if the angels set down their bowling balls and hurled the rain at us between frames. We got back in the truck; two passengers still in the back. Leonardo, Claudia, and I looked at the rain as it pounded the windshield. "Man!" exclaimed Leonardo. "I *knew* I should have rewired the wipers in this thing."

Leonardo drove with his head out the window because it was pointless to look through the windshield. Here's something I didn't know about driving in mud of Sonora desert clay: it's like driving on ice. We slipped and fishtailed, going sideways as much as we went forward, except unlike driving on ice, we didn't slide into snow banks; we crashed into mesquite instead, and sometimes we drove right over the bushes. We sloshed through the swollen streams which had been dry an hour before. Water was everywhere. At first I felt guilty about taking my seat in the front, while others got soaked in the truck bed behind, but the cab with its open windows wasn't affording all that much protection. When we got to the gate demarcating our return to the ranch road, Leonardo drew his soaked head back inside the truck and grinned at me. "I'm from Oregon. I love the rain."

By the time we rattled and bumped and splashed and slid our way down the ranch road, the arroyo that had been our path to the border certainly would be filled with water. The flood would have erased the puma's paw prints, covered the empty pants with an extra layer of silt, and washed the dung beetle alongside uncountable bits of debris, northward into the United States, an unnoticed illegal entry. I wondered if maybe this was the rush of water that would topple the fence once more, leaving "a gap where even two could walk abreast."

It was good to look north across the border during the desert's rainy season, because water and migration have a lot in common. It is nearly impossible to stop water as it flows downhill. With a lot of effort and some well-informed hydrological engineering, water can be detained for a time in dams and in reservoirs; water can be diverted using a well-made ditch or canal, but water always flows downhill. It always finds its destination. Something similar can be said for the migration of people. When economic need, warfare, or family ties make the crossing of borders necessary, those borders will be crossed.

There is no structure built by human hands that cannot be dismantled by human hands. Walls are expensive, ladders are cheap, and besides, nature seems to side with the immigrant, at least where I visited the wall. Nor is there is any evidence that the growing wall along the border has stemmed the tide of migration, though it has changed the nature of migration. When I first visited Douglas and Agua Prieta in 1996, the border was demarcated by two strands of barbed wire. It was easy to cross and people did so all of the time.

Now the same people must go out into the desert where it's infinitely more dangerous. They risk exposure to the cold in winter and to heat and flash floods during the summer. They spend great sums of money for the privilege of placing themselves at the mercy of guides—*coyotes* or *polleros*—who have a well-deserved reputation for dishonesty. Those who cannot afford *coyotes* often turn to the *narcos* for help. The drug traffickers are willing to help migrants cross the border on the condition that those heading north will carry heavy backpacks full of marijuana, cocaine, or crystal meth to eager customers in the United States.

Before visiting the Sonora desert I spoke about the border wall with Julia Thorne, an immigration lawyer employed by the Presbyterian Church (U.S.A.). She described the immigration enforcement along the U.S./Mexico border as a disastrous mess.

> It used to be that people could cross into the United States seasonably to do various kinds of temporary labor, especially in agriculture. But now they've built this wall, and they've stepped up enforcement, so people have had to get *coyotes*, human smugglers, to help them get across. At first these coyotes just smuggled people, and that was OK, but then the drug cartels saw that the *coyotes* were making money and were good at getting people across the border and they wanted in on the action. They started forcing the *coyotes* to smuggle drugs, and the situation ratcheted up, and things got much, much worse.
>
> Now the men couldn't cross back after a season's work, and so they started paying for their families to come north. So now you have families, women and children going across, getting involved in the mess along the border.

When we reached the main highway that would take us back into town, the rain had subsided to a drizzle. Leonardo stopped the pickup, but with the engine still running he popped the hood and opened the radiator cap. He poured several quarts of water down into the radiator, and we rattled our way out onto the open road.

Ten minutes down the highway we saw a white taxicab pulled over onto the gravel beyond the shoulder. "That's how they get out here—taxis—and look. There they go." Leonardo gestured to a group of women running into the mesquite, heading through the desert toward the American border. "Those women will end up where we were. I'm glad we left some water for them. I hope they make it."

Amen.

Two months after he took me out into the desert, I tried to contact Leonardo. The director of CRREDA told me that Leonardo had left the program. "*Salió por problemas familiares*"—he left because of family problems—is all the information I got, but it says a lot. All of Leonardo's family members live north of the border. If Leonardo left Mexico to be with them, it is likely that he traveled through the desert in the places he knew best, out where he'd driven his beat-up pickup to leave water for migrants, perhaps down the arroyo to where he knew the border fence was likely to wash out in a flash flood.

I hope he made it across. If he was thirsty, I hope he found water left by a soul as kind as he is. If, in the wilderness, he faced serious hardship, I hope the ghost of Toribio Romo or some lesser saint who could recognize Christ in the face of a wayfaring neighbor was able to show him the way home.

Chapter 9

Liliana and the New Sanctuary Movement

We have met the enemy and [s]he is us.

—Walt Kelly, creator of Pogo

During the summer of 2007, "Save Our State," an organization that calls itself a "home to grassroots activists fighting illegal immigration" and is classified as a hate group by the Southern Poverty Law Center,[1] began weekly protests on the sidewalk in front of the United Church of Christ in Simi Valley, California, a predominantly white and Republican enclave north of Los Angeles that is home to the Ronald Reagan Presidential Library. Before long, members of groups with names like "Americans for Legal Immigration," "Stop the Invasion," "Mothers Against Illegal Immigration," joined an assortment of unaffiliated "minutemen," self-described patriots, and a few neo-Nazis in the protests.

On Sunday mornings while the congregation worshiped, the protesters gathered to decry the presence of Liliana, an undocumented immigrant, who, having received deportation orders, sought and received sanctuary from the United Church of Christ in Simi Valley.

The protests continued each week for a year with blaring bullhorns and signs proclaiming, almost poetically:

UNCHECKED
IMMIGRATION
A WILDFIRE
THAT WILL CONSUME
OUR NATION
STOP THE INVASION

And

> WAR IS PEACE
> FREEDOM IS SLAVERY
> IGNORANCE IS STRENGTH
> IMMIGRATION IS GREAT
> IT'S TIME TO
> WAKE UP!
> STOP ILLEGAL
> IMMIGRATION

And, more prosaically:

> DON'T
> Attend this
> LAWBREAKER
> CHURCH![2]

At times there were counter protestors, and both groups lodged accusations of violence and provocation against one another. In preparation for the final protest on July 27, 2008 (according to my sources, they quit simply because they got tired of organizing the protests), Save Our State issued the following press release:

> It is Americans who now need "sanctuary" from criminal aliens who are killing our children (Jamiel Shaw[3]), taking our jobs, terrorizing our schools, destroying our economy, and joining dangerous gangs and drug cartels.
>
> Liliana, the corrupt church, and the Simi Valley government are symbols of the lawless invasion and terrorism of our nation. So please join us on Sunday July 27th!! Let's return and ask the city officials, ICE, and the church why they continue to defy our laws and put Americans in harm's way!!![4]

On a hot summer day, almost a year after the protests ended, I traveled to Simi Valley with Alice Linsmeier, an organizer from the New Sanctuary Movement, to meet Liliana in the parsonage where she lives on the grounds of the United Church of Christ. One of the church's former pastors, the Rev. Frank Johnson, met us at the door, ushered us into the house, and introduced me to the woman who, according to her detractors, is a "criminal alien." According to Save Our State, Liliana is responsible for "killing our children, taking our jobs, terrorizing our schools, destroying our economy, and joining dangerous gangs and drug cartels."

She was making iced tea.

Liliana—who doesn't disclose her last name—is a small woman with kind eyes and a bright smile. On the day I visited, her three children—ages nine, six, and two—were with her, and her love for them was palpable. It was hard for me to imagine how this family was anything like a "wildfire that will consume our nation," nor did she appear a particularly intimidating invader. Mostly, she just seemed like the kind of energetic parent who would, under different circumstances, volunteer as the den mother in her son's Cub Scout troop; she would bring cookies and all of the Scouts would be smitten with her.

When she was a high school student in a small town in the Mexican state of Michoacan, Liliana's parents, along with her ten brothers and sisters, applied for and received visas to move to the United States. Liliana chose to stay behind to finish high school and to earn a degree in psychology from a university in Morelia, the state capitol of Michoacan.

Liliana graduated from high school in 1996, at a time when Mexico's economy was enduring a post-NAFTA contraction. The value of the peso was plummeting, and while Liliana found work at a small store in her hometown, it was impossible to earn enough money for her university education. About the same time, she applied for a tourist visa, hoping to visit her parents in Oxnard, California, where they had settled after moving north. Her application for a tourist visa was unsuccessful.

With no prospects for an education in Mexico and faced with the possibility of being unable to see her parents, Liliana decided to cross the border without papers. Her plan was to work for a year while living with her parents, and, during that year, to save enough money to finance her university education in Mexico. (Unlike in America, a Mexican university education can be financed on the earnings of an undocumented immigrant.)

And so it was that in December of 1998, Liliana met up with her parents and one of her brothers—all in possession of legal papers that enabled them to cross the border at will—in Tijuana, Baja California, at the northwest tip of Mexico. Liliana's parents, being unable to risk their own legal status by smuggling her across the border, hired a *coyote* for Liliana, and she was ready to cross into the United States under the *coyote's* direction.

Initially, the *coyote* told Liliana and her family that he would drive her across the border using a false residency card, but after her family left her alone with the *coyote*, he changed his mind.

Instead, the *coyote* sent Liliana to the border on foot in the company of his thirteen-year-old niece. He gave Liliana a "document" to present to the inspection officer. "Learn the information on the way to the border," he directed, "and when you get to the officials at the border, tell them it's your paper." Liliana did not know what the document was, but according to the *coyote*, it would get her across the border.

Liliana knew it was a bad idea, but she felt trapped. She could not turn back and she couldn't contact her family. "I didn't have any option," Liliana told me, "I didn't know anyone in Tijuana, and I didn't know what else to do. I was nervous, and when I got to the inspection at the border I was crying, and that was it. I was taken to secondary inspection for interrogation. I told the officers who I was, and that I didn't know what document I was presenting to them. They detained me and sent me back to Mexico."

At the time Liliana was nineteen years old, and what she attempted, under duress from her *coyote*, was not all that different from what many American nineteen-year-olds attempt when, in search of underage inebriation, they want to buy beer. Showing false documents to an immigration officer is a felony, however, an indiscretion serious enough that Liliana is permanently barred from entry into the United States. At the time, she was unaware of this detail, which plays an important part later in her story.

After spending an additional month in Tijuana, Liliana was able to cross the border successfully in the Arizona desert and to make her way safely to Oxnard, California, just north of Los Angeles, where she moved in with her parents and found work at a corn-packing plant.

Liliana found more than work at the corn-packing plant. She also met a coworker named Gerardo and found love. "That was 1998," Liliana recalled with a smile, "and I changed my plan to return to Mexico to study psychology." Liliana and Gerardo were married and, in 2000, their eldest son was born. Three years later they had a daughter, and they were happy.

As the family grew, Gerardo completed the process to become a naturalized American citizen, and in 2004 Liliana, now the wife and mother of American citizens, became a legal resident of the United States. She applied for and received a work permit, a social security number, and a driver's license. Encouraged by her work permit and knowing no reason not to continue down the path to citizenship in the country she now called home, Liliana applied for permanent residence.

Although her record had apparently eluded the Department of Homeland Security when she applied for a work permit, the fact that Liliana had been arrested for using a false document several years before came to the attention of the people who processed her request for residency. She met with officials expecting to be welcomed as a permanent resident. Instead, the Department of Homeland Security gave her a deportation order.

But Liliana didn't leave. She and Gerardo told the officials about their children and explained that it would hardly work for Gerardo to commute from Tijuana to his two jobs in Oxnard. (It's a good five hours from Tijuana to Oxnard, and that's only if traffic in Los Angeles is light, which it never is.) The officials relented. "Tell you what," the couple was told, "we're going to be good people. Leave this building and don't ever come back. When your work permit expires don't reapply because if you ever come back other people may not have the heart that we have and you will be deported."

Liliana and Gerardo were scared, but grateful that Liliana had not been deported. They began the work of trying to find a legal way to keep the family together in Oxnard. They retained the services of an immigration lawyer, but the laws governing immigration offer no flexibility. The only advice the lawyer could give her was, "Give thanks to God that you weren't deported. Most people would not even have been able to go home to Oxnard."

In search of a second opinion, Liliana and Gerardo went to another lawyer who agreed with the first. "It's a miracle you are still here. Your only option is to wait for a change in the law." Liliana was not welcome in the United States.

For a while returning to the shadows to live the life of an undocumented immigrant worked for Liliana. She kept working and before too long she and her husband were able to make a down payment on a house where they moved in 2005. A third child—a son—was born, and life seemed good. The Department of Homeland Security made no effort to contact her, so she assumed they had forgotten about her or had better things to do. But on March 16, 2007, two months after her third child's birth, Liliana awoke to an early morning phone call from Gerardo, who had just left for work.

"The police are outside the house and they're asking for you," he said. "Can you come out and talk with them?" Barefoot, dressed in pajamas, and still on the phone with her husband, Liliana looked outside her window. The officers in front of her house wore bulletproof vests marked with the letters "ICE," which stands for "Immigration and Customs Enforcement."

"That's not the Oxnard Police," Liliana told her husband. "That's *la migra*."

Five officers entered her house and told her to get ready to leave. "What about my kids?" she asked.

"We're sorry. We've come for you. Your husband will have to watch the kids."

By this time Gerardo was back in the house, and he protested, "I don't have time to watch the kids. I'm working two jobs to pay the mortgage."

"Well," an ICE officer responded, "you're a citizen and your children are citizens. You can go visit your wife in Tijuana on the weekends."

Gerardo shot back, "Do you think Tijuana is just down the block?" But before the conversation could degenerate any further, the children interrupted. First, Liliana and Gerardo's two-month-old son began to cry in the bedroom. The sound of an infant came as a surprise to the ICE agents, who did not know that a third child had been added to the family. Second, Liliana's four-year-old daughter came into the kitchen, saw her mother crying, and began to plead with one of the ICE agents who was a woman.

"Why are you taking my *mami?*" came the words of a precocious preschooler. "My *mami* is a good *mami*. She cooks for me, she helps me with my homework. Why are you taking my *mami*? Why?"

The ICE agent had no reply.

Gerardo left to get his crying son and came back holding the baby. He continued interrogating the ICE agent.

"What would you do in my situation? I have a two-month-old baby who needs his mother. I have a four-year-old and a six-year-old. What would you do?"

"I understand, and I'm sorry," said the officer, "but I have to take her with me."

But Liliana and Gerardo were persistent, and after some negotiating, it was decided that Liliana would be given a week to make arrangements, get ready, and turn herself in to the Immigration and Customs Enforcement offices in Camarillo.

Liliana and Gerardo began to explore options, and after a discouraging meeting with a sympathetic immigration lawyer, they began to look into the possibility of finding sanctuary for Liliana.

Sanctuary Movements, Old and New

Sanctuary is a concept rooted in the biblical mandate that among the cities of ancient Israel certain communities would be designated as "sanctuary cities." The purpose of such cities was to provide accused murderers with a reprieve from a swift miscarriage of mob justice. An accused murderer able to reach a sanctuary city had time to prove that he or she was not, in fact, guilty of premeditated murder, but of a lesser offense such as manslaughter or killing in self-defense. In the Christian era, the concept of sanctuary was expanded to apply to all Roman Catholic churches in medieval Europe, and while American law does not formally recognize sanctuary provided by churches and other religious institutions, such sanctuary often is informally respected.

The New Sanctuary Movement is a revival of a movement that began in the 1980s as a way of sheltering undocumented refugees from Central America. During the 1980s, as desperately violent civil wars raged in the region, tens of thousands of refugees moved north from El Salvador, Nicaragua, and Guatemala to escape the bloodshed rending their homelands.

Most of the refugees who ended up in the United States—especially those from El Salvador and Guatemala—were undocumented because, although the United States has a proud history of welcoming and settling those who qualify as refugees under international law, the governments and armed forces of El Salvador and Guatemala were fighting proxy wars on behalf of the United States. These wars were bankrolled almost entirely by United States taxpayers, and the United States found it inconvenient to acknowledge the humanitarian crisis caused by its violent foreign policies.

For many of the refugees who found their way north, a return to their homes would have been a sentence of death, so to help preserve the lives of those who might be deported, faith communities in the United States began offering sanctuary for those in greatest danger. Eventually, more than five hundred churches and religious communities participated in the eighties-era sanctuary movement, which ended as the Central American conflicts resolved themselves after the end of the Cold War.

In January of 2007, in the face of a growing trend toward increasingly draconian enforcement of immigration laws, a coalition of religious leaders from sixteen denominations and religious traditions from twelve different cities around the United States met in Washington, D.C. to discuss possibilities for a broad-based religious response to the needs of immigrants suffering under tougher regulations and stricter enforcement. Thus began the "New Sanctuary Movement."

Although it has affiliate networks in at least ten states, the movement remains, as one organizer put it, "an open-source movement" that manifests itself in a variety of ways in different places. But in every place the goal of the New Sanctuary Movement is, according to charter member Alice Linsmeier, "to awaken the moral imagination of the United States." Linsmeier attended the January 2007 meeting at which the New Sanctuary Movement was born, and in March of that year, her employer, the local branch of an organization called Clergy and Laity United for Economic Justice (CLUE), decided to embrace the sanctuary movement.

CLUE is a California-based interfaith network whose stated goal is "to end low-wage poverty in California by building a faith-rooted movement for economic justice throughout the state" through advocacy in areas of human rights and migrant rights.[5] From the beginning, CLUE chapters around California have been integral in the development of the New Sanctuary Movement, and the Ventura County chapter of CLUE was involved and supportive. At first, however, the Ventura County CLUE's decision to participate in the New Sanctuary Movement did not include a commitment to become involved with housing anyone. Theirs was a dedication to prayer, education, and helping other faith communities discern their involvement in the movement.

That changed in May of 2007, just two months after CLUE decided to participate in the New Sanctuary Movement, when Liliana came looking for sanctuary. "She forced our hand," Alice Linsmeier told me. "It was like a *Posadas*." The *Posadas* is a traditional musical drama that reenacts the story of Joseph and Mary seeking a place to stay in Bethlehem, Mary being great with child. Facing such a moral dilemma and looking toward biblical precedent, CLUE changed its policy and became directly involved in providing housing and sanctuary.

Sanctuary in Action

When Liliana and Gerardo set out to find sanctuary in a church, they didn't know what it meant exactly to receive sanctuary. "I had heard about sanctuary on television, but I didn't really know what it was, except that they protected people," she told me. Liliana and Gerardo's lawyer put them in touch with Alice Linsmeier, who made arrangements to meet the couple. Before meeting with Alice, Liliana still wasn't convinced sanctuary was the right program for her. She visited the Mexican consulate in Los Angeles and met with a community group that assists migrants with their paperwork, but no one could help her. It became clear that sanctuary was her only option if Liliana wanted to stay in the United States.

When Liliana and Gerardo first met with Alice, there were no churches in the community willing to provide sanctuary for Liliana. They went first to the local Roman Catholic church, but the priest felt he was unable to help. Instead, he sent Liliana to a community of nuns who, twenty years before, had offered sanctuary to refugees from El Salvador and Guatemala. The nuns, unfortunately, had gotten out of the sanctuary business when the Cold War ended, after things calmed down in Central America. They said they were unable to provide a safe place for Liliana, but Alice Linsmeier was persistent. "We'll find a place for you," she promised, and eventually they did.

In fact, over time the New Sanctuary Movement found three places for Liliana and her infant son. First, they stayed in the home of a Roman Catholic deacon and his wife in Sierra Madre, east of Pasadena, in the foothills north of Los Angeles, but the transition into sanctuary wasn't an easy one. "It was sad. Very sad," Liliana told me. Liliana and Gerardo had a fairly traditional distribution of domestic responsibilities, meaning he worked two jobs outside the home, and she worked one job and was almost entirely responsible for running the household. Gerardo didn't know how to cook and since the early days of their marriage, he had never paid a bill. He didn't know how to run the washing machine.

Liliana packed her bags, stocked the kitchen with food and a few prepared meals, and taught her husband how to balance the checkbook and operate a washing machine. As Liliana told me about this time of separation, her youngest son crawled up into her lap, and buried his head in her chest. For the first time, more than half an hour into our interview, Liliana got emotional. We all got emotional—Alice, Frank, and me—and that's as it should be, I suppose. After all, the forced separation of a young woman from her husband and two of her children is, fundamentally, painful. It's the kind of pain that transcends politics and theological proclivities, but when it is touched by grace it can be redemptive. It can strip us of the burdens of bias and prejudice that we all carry with us and make us more human by connecting us to the image of God in which we were made—the image of a God who, according to the Christian story, is intimately familiar with the pain experienced when a parent is separated from her child.

Liliana spent three weeks in Sierra Madre, where she received a warm welcome from the Catholic community, including visits by and supportive letters from two auxiliary bishops from the Archdiocese of Los Angeles. From Sierra Madre she moved into a converted office space at St. Luke's Episcopal Church in Long Beach, where she stayed for three months.

In Long Beach the protests began. In the New Sanctuary Movement, prophetic witness is part of the deal. Those who provide sanctuary and those who receive it agree to participate in prophetic witness by being open about what is being provided, who is being helped, and why. Liliana and the New Sanctuary Movement sought and received publicity about the help Liliana was receiving. A variety of local and regional news media ran stories about Liliana's plight, and on July 8, 2007, the story of Liliana's protection under the New Sanctuary Movement was splashed across the front page of *USA Today*.[6]

Through the publicity generated by Liliana's presence at Saint Luke's Episcopal Church in Long Beach, various anti-immigration activist groups became aware of Liliana's story and began to organize protests outside of St. Luke's. These same types of protests would later follow Liliana to Simi Valley.

During one of the early protests, Liliana's children asked her what was going on, and why they wanted Liliana deported. "Are they bad people?" asked Liliana's daughter.

"No, *mija*, they just don't want me here."

"Doesn't that make them bad?" asked her oldest son.

"No," replied Liliana. "They just think they're saving the state."

"*Mami*, don't they have jobs?"

"Probably not, *mijita*."

The protestors believe they kicked Liliana out of Long Beach, but according to Liliana, she left Long Beach because she wanted to be closer to her family. She remembers:

> It was hard in Long Beach. I could only see my family on the weekends, and sometimes it was harder when they came. Some weeks they could stay all weekend long, but other times my husband would have to work on Saturday and they wouldn't get to Long Beach until ten or eleven at night. Then they'd have to leave Sunday afternoon because Gerardo had to wake up early for work. It was hard on all of us.
>
> The kids were traumatized; they looked like they weren't getting enough to eat. My daughter started trying to convince me to come home. "We'll put a bigger peep hole in the door so we can look out to see who comes to our door, and if it's *la migra* we won't open up and if they come in anyway, you can hide under the bed or maybe you can wear a wig and they won't know you.

> If they ask me I'll tell them you don't live here. They won't do anything to me because I'm just a little girl."

It was time for Liliana to move closer to home.

Alice Linsmeier approached the board of Ventura County CLUE about Liliana's need for a place closer to home. A new board member, The Rev. Dr. June Goudey, had recently become the pastor of the Simi Valley United Church of Christ. Her congregation owned an old manse that was located on the church's property. The manse was vacant and in need of serious repair, but it seemed worth it to approach the congregation to see if they wanted to be a sanctuary congregation and to extend the hospitality of sacred space to Liliana.

In Simi Valley, at the United Church of Christ, being a "New Sanctuary Congregation" meant welcoming Liliana. I asked the Rev. Frank Johnson, a former copastor at Simi Valley United Church of Christ, what inspired the congregation to open the doors of its manse to a woman who, besides being pursued by Immigration and Customs Enforcement, also was a complete stranger.

As Frank sees it, the welcome of Liliana began long before sanctuary was on the mind of anyone at the church—or, more properly, the churches. The Simi Valley United Church of Christ is the product of two congregations, one in Simi Valley and the other in nearby Thousand Oaks. Both congregations were struggling to find ways to express a welcome for gays and lesbians while living and worshiping in what safely can be described as one of California's most politically and theologically conservative communities.

A mutual desire to extend a welcome to gays and lesbians drew the two congregations together. Eventually, they merged, selling the property in Thousand Oaks and rebuilding the sanctuary in Simi Valley.

"By the time we came together we were pretty well united in the welcoming and acceptance of gay and lesbian people, and so that kind of set the tone for us as we began to consider what our mission was in this area here in Simi Valley," Frank explained.

After Frank and his copastor retired, Jane Goudey, the woman currently serving as pastor to Simi Valley United Church of Christ, became involved in progressive religious causes in Ventura County. After hearing about an early morning ICE raid, such as the one endured by Liliana and her family, she began talking with church members about offering the church's manse as a place of refuge and sanctuary. A series of meetings were held, and in July of 2007, the congregation voted to become a sanctuary church.

> By this time the support was not unanimous, but it was overwhelming, and so we were pretty well united in our decision and our calling to express our caring for the community in this way, partly because in the UCC we have this slogan, "God is still speaking." We felt that if God is still speaking and we are offering an extravagant welcome, then in order to live this out we needed to take this step. We felt called to it.

After meeting Liliana and her family, the congregation invited her to move north.

Liliana arrived in Simi Valley late on an August night in 2007. When we met nearly two years later, she had not yet left the property of the United Church of Christ. She lives in the parsonage, which has been divided into two dwellings—one for Liliana and the other for the new pastor Jane Goudey and her partner. On Sundays Liliana worships with the small congregation. She works, as she is able with limited English, in the church office and she helps the janitor who cleans the church facility once a week. Mostly she waits for laws to change, so that she can have her life back, so that she can live in her home, with her husband and children. Someday she'd even like to earn her long-deferred degree in psychology—she's seen the positive effect of therapy in the lives of her children and she'd like to make helping others her life's work. But for now she waits. It's an undertaking that requires great patience and emotional endurance, but right now it's all she can do.

Before concluding the interview, I asked Liliana if she had any final words for those who would one day read about her in the book you now have in your hand. "I give thanks to God for everyone who has supported me," she said. "And those who want me deported, I don't think they are racists, but if people would learn more, if they would take time to read about immigrants and what we're like, maybe they wouldn't be so hard on us." It's a fair enough request.

She left me with one last story.

> I remember one night, not long before *la migra* came for the first time. I was brushing my teeth, thinking about how lucky I was to have a husband who loved me and three beautiful children, and I asked God if this was it. "Is this all I'm supposed to do with my life or is there more? What is my function?" And if you look at the whole story it's like a jigsaw puzzle, it all fits together, and I'm asking God if He wants me to be the voice of undocumented immigrants while the government reforms the immigration system. There are so many families being separated. Something has to be done. I'm asking God why He's chosen me, and He'll tell me some day.

Later, as we reflected on Liliana's story, Alice Linsmeier told me, "The level of Liliana and Gerardo's faith shakes me to the bones. It harkens back to the Old Testament prophets and to the great people of the Christian story. Faith is what keeps them going. People who know Liliana and Gerardo are transformed by their faith."

As we drove out of Simi Valley it occurred to me that Liliana may be a lot of things: mother, undocumented immigrant, spokesperson for twelve million other undocumented immigrants, or great woman of faith. Whatever she is, her presence in the United States seems to pose no risk to the security of the homeland.

Chapter 10

Good *Escuelas en la* 'Hood: Immigrants and School

School and shoes and food and books, believin' in a prayer
God must know His way 'round on the west side of town.
—Tish Hinojosa, "West Side of Town,"
from the album Homeland

On her first day of kindergarten, my daughter met Preston Smith at the door to the school cafeteria. At the time, Preston was in his third year working as the principal of the small, autonomous, inner-city elementary school where my daughter was enrolled as a student. He greeted her with a grin, gave her a high five, and, addressing her by her name, told her to tuck in her shirt. "You've got to dress for success," he told her. Since that day my daughter's shirttails have not seen the outside of her pants at school.

For his part, Preston Smith was wearing gabardine slacks, a pink shirt and a purple tie. Evidently this is the wardrobe choice of a successful urban principal, because Preston Smith has had more than his share of success working with immigrant children as an inner-city educator.

Mr. Smith—as he is known to his students—first came to the largely Hispanic and immigrant Alum Rock School district in East San José, California as part of the Teach for America program, an organization that seeks to place highly skilled, recent college graduates and professionals in underperforming schools around the country. His initial plan was to spend a few years teaching and paying off student loans before heading to law school, but life, or perhaps divine intervention, came between him and a legal career. Mr. Smith is still educating at-risk students, many of whom come from poor, immigrant backgrounds.

As a member of the Teach for America corps, Mr. Smith quickly established himself as one of the best teachers in San José, and because of his excellence in the classroom, a local faith-based community organizing group asked him to be the founding principal of a small, innovative, autonomous public school called LUCHA (an acronym for "Learning in an Urban Community with High Achievement"; the word *lucha* is Spanish for fight). Nearly all of Mr. Smith's students at LUCHA came from low-income households. Most of the students at LUCHA were English-language learners, the children of immigrants, and often immigrants themselves. Frequently the children and their families resided in the United States without documentation. Almost none of the parents were college-educated, and many hadn't even completed high school.

Preston Smith's students at LUCHA came from a demographic that is challenging to educators. Studies show that the students least likely to succeed in American schools are poor children of uneducated immigrant parents, children who have not learned English at home.[1] These are the students that Mr. Smith's school aimed to educate.

A combination of rigorous academics, strong teaching from enthusiastic teachers, and a positive, nurturing atmosphere made the school a success. Within three years Mr. Smith's students' standardized test scores were better than any other public elementary school in San José, and were on a par with wealthier communities in the Bay Area such as Palo Alto (home to Stanford University and Hewlett Packard) and Cupertino (a city that is home to Apple Computer and boasts some of the best public schools in the state).

After my daughter's kindergarten year, Preston Smith left LUCHA, but he continued working in educational reform. He went to work for a organization called Rocketship Education, described on its Web site as "a non-profit company dedicated to eliminating the achievement gap between low-income and middle-class students."[2] Smith's new job was to help Rocketship design and establish charter schools in San José's predominantly immigrant neighborhoods. When I met with Preston Smith in the summer of 2009 for lunch at a wonderfully decrepit Mexican restaurant in downtown San José, the first Rocketship charter school had just finished its second year with scores on standardized math tests that ranked Mr. Smith's second graders—almost all of them poor, immigrant students who did not have English as a first language—at an astonishing seventh best among second graders in all of California. The second Rocketship charter school was just months from opening its doors, with a third planned for the fall of 2010.

Preston Smith had just turned thirty.

Though he is a lifelong Presbyterian whose work is sustained by prayer, Preston Smith's career as an educator was, at first, motivated less by his own faith than by the faithfulness of the ecumenical and interfaith community in San José whose efforts helped lead the educational reform movement in the area.

When I asked Preston how his own faith motivated him in his work as an educator he replied,

> Mostly it's a matter of justice. I grew up in Rialto, in Southern California. It's a tough neighborhood where there was a lot of gang violence and urban decay—it wasn't the hard-core inner city, but my neighborhood faced a lot of the same issues you might see in the urban core.
>
> I graduated second in my high school class of a thousand students. I was the student body president. I played soccer and was on the mock trial team. I was a good student, the kind of kid who should have gotten into any college I wanted, but when I applied to UCLA as my safety school, I didn't get in. Some of my friends who were athletes got in, but not me.
>
> When I called the dean of admissions to find out why I had been rejected, they told me it was because of my high school. They assumed that my grades were inflated because I was from Rialto, and besides, I'm a white male, and the school told me that if they were going to take a white male they'd find him from a better high school.
>
> What I learned then is that your opportunities in life can be limited by your zip code, and I want to make sure that my students won't be limited because of where they live. I want them to attend schools with such a strong reputation that the very best colleges and universities will be happy to give them a shot.

An important component of Preston Smith's educational approach is that teachers should be familiar with each student's home life.

Every semester, each Rocketship student is visited at home. "The conditions in which some of these kids are being raised are unimaginable," Preston told me, "and what's amazing is that for many of these families this is part of a greater dream for the children's future. It is truly humbling to think about what my students' parents have sacrificed so that their kids could have a decent education. They left their homes and extended families, many of them, and they made an often dangerous crossing into America so that their kids could have hope for a better life. It is humbling, and I know that I have to honor that sacrifice as an educator."

Preston Smith is a man of humble, thoughtful faith, and as we finished up our enchiladas and parted ways—he back to his school and I back to my church—I was struck by how well his vocational calling gives expression to his religious convictions. In many ways he models the Calvinist ideal of ministry being the work of all Christians who seek to glorify God in the work they do. If asked, "Who is my neighbor?" I have no doubt Preston Smith would tell you the story of a child whose parents took great risk to cross borders that were both geopolitical and societal, about how honoring that sacrifice means providing their children with an excellent education regardless of the neighborhood they call home.

Education for All: The Challenges

Of course, if it were easy to provide a quality education to the children of immigrants, Preston Smith's achievements as an educator would be unremarkable, but educating immigrant children is not easy. I asked Tom Luschei, a professor of comparative international education policy at Florida State University, to help me understand the difficulties involved in providing a quality education for immigrant children. Before he began teaching at Florida State, Tom earned his PhD from Stanford, where he wrote his dissertation on educational policy in Mexico. Prior to that, he taught immigrants at the elementary and high school levels in the Los Angeles Unified School District. Tom's wife, Yasmín, who immigrated to the United States from Mexico when she was a child, is a bilingual elementary school teacher. Understandably, the education of immigrant children is something about which Tom is passionate.

I asked Tom which challenges were most difficult for those seeking to educate immigrants.

> Language is a big issue. That's sort of obvious and everyone likes to talk about language. It's been the focus of policymaking for a long time, but there's more than that. Kids are being alienated in our schools. They've been uprooted from their home environments; they've been taken from a place of high social capital and they've been thrust into a place of very low social capital. This leads to a sense of isolation.
>
> Often the newly arrived kids show up with a strong desire to succeed in school. They reflect their parents' drive to achieve the American dream. In fact, the first generation immigrant children often do better than second or third generation kids, but it's hard to keep that desire for success alive.
>
> When I was teaching elementary school in East Los Angeles, I would have kids show up from Mexico or Central America, and they'd be great students, eager to please their teacher, but for their efforts they were teased by the American kids. Over time you could see the immigrant kids lose their drive.

Another challenge is that the schools themselves are often failing. "Immigrants from Latin America often end up in poor, inner-city schools. Often they suffer from substandard teaching and from facilities that are falling apart, and it's hard to help undocumented parents understand that they can demand better for their children."

Tom thought for a moment, and asked me, "Who is more disenfranchised than an immigrant kid whose parents are undocumented?"

Finding ways to get immigrant parents involved in the education system is also a big challenge for educators in immigrant communities. "I think parent involvement is a very important issue," Tom told me, "particularly since there is such an enormous power, culture, and knowledge gap between immigrant parents and their children's teachers and schools. At a parent-teacher conference I once lectured a Guatemalan father for ten minutes on his daughter's problems with *lectura* (reading) and how he needed to practice '*lectura*' with her every day. He listened to me patiently, and once I had finished, I asked if he had any questions. 'Just one, maestro. *¿Qué es lectura?* (What is reading?)'

"I draw the analogy with my own involvement as a parent of a daughter who is now taking ballet lessons. I know as much about ballet as my Guatemalan student's father knew about *lectura.* I can show up and watch my daughter take her lessons, but I have no clue whether she is doing it well or even if she is in the ballpark. But immigrant parents also have to deal with language, cultural misunderstandings, immigration status, social disenfranchisement, discrimination, etc. In order to get parents like this involved and active in their children's education, teachers and schools are going to have to make serious efforts, and make it very clear that they don't care about documents."

Organizing for Stronger Schools in the Community

The empowerment of parents, giving them ownership in their children's education, has been the defining characteristic of the educational reform movement in East San José, where Preston Smith's work has borne such fruit. I met with Matt Hammer, an organizer with PACT (an acronym for People Acting in Community Together), a faith-based community organization, whose work in East San José sparked the educational reform movement in which Preston Smith is working and in which my own children are being educated.

Matt Hammer comes from one of San José's important political families. His father was the president of the San José Unified School District's school board and his mother was San José's mayor during the halcyon days of Silicon Valley's dot-com boom. But he credits his political passions to experiences he had as a student at Duke University, where he helped to organize a community service center that encouraged Duke students and faculty to become more involved in the community. After graduation Matt became the director of the center, and through that work he came into contact with community organizers in Durham who encouraged him to think about educational reform.

When I met with Matt in a converted Sunday school room on the second floor of a local Presbyterian church where PACT has offices,

Matt told me about his experiences in Durham. "These organizers were always poking at me saying, 'It doesn't matter how many Duke students you send into the Durham public schools, they're always going to be a mess until the people in Durham demand and create better schools,' so that eventually got in my craw and I decided I wanted to learn what organizing was about."

Matt worked as an organizer in Mississippi and later in Oakland, California before coming home to San José to work for PACT, and everywhere he has organized, educational reform has been a priority for him. I asked him why education had played such an important role in his work as an organizer, and in part, his involvement in educational reform is inspired by his personal story. As a child, Matt attended public schools in San José, where he was among a small minority of white students, and where he received support and was encouraged to succeed in school and to go on to college. Most of Matt's classmates, however, did not get such encouragement or support.

"I've come to understand that the schools were set up to allow someone like me to go to college," he told me, "but in my graduating class, in 1986, there were 5 percent of us—most of us white—who went on to four-year schools, but the majority of the students in the school were Latino. No one saw that as a big problem."

Except, of course, that the parents saw the system as a problem. In his work as an organizer, Matt quickly discovered that while most parents felt powerless to change their children's schools, none of the parents were satisfied with the kind of system that is set up to allow white kids to succeed while minority kids fail. He told me, "I've asked hundreds of parents, 'What are your dreams for your kids?' and everybody says they want their kids to have more options than they had. They want their kids to go to university. They want their kids to have a career. And there's this cold shower that often comes for an immigrant when their kid becomes a middle schooler or a late-elementary schooler, and they realize that something is going terribly wrong with their kid's education."

So PACT began the work of organizing parents to fix what was wrong with the educational system in the Alum Rock School District in San José's East Side. In 2000 organizers from PACT started meeting with parents at Our Lady of Guadalupe Catholic Church. Most of the parents had children attending nearby Cesar Chavez[3] Elementary

School. "This group of moms was dissatisfied with what was going on at that school," Matt told me. "It was a huge mess."

The parents organized by PACT met and developed a plan of action that involved holding a large meeting in the sanctuary of their church. They invited the superintendent and members of the school board to attend the meeting and at the meeting they challenged them publicly to fix the school's problems.

It worked. The superintendent and the school board promised to address a wide range of issues, including nonfunctioning, disgustingly dirty bathrooms, high staff turnover, and a lack of textbooks.

> Once parents saw that they could move the system and have some success they started asking other questions. So we got the bathrooms cleaned up, but what is the real purpose of Cesar Chavez school? It's to educate our kids, but what kind of education do we want? Let's look at the statistics and find out how the school is doing on that score. Does the state think Chavez is doing a good job? It was a long process.
>
> We deliberately wanted these efforts to be grounded in congregations because immigrant parents often don't feel like they have any secular community institutions they can own and trust, but they have the church, so through church we were able to pull people together fairly effectively and to get people to speak together fairly honestly with relatively little fear.
>
> So we'd build community among these parents in the church context. Church leaders would come in and would support these efforts and the parents would see that they weren't on their own and that the hierarchy of the church was supporting them and praying for them, and was willing to stand with them in this struggle that was coming.

In 2002, after some initial successes, PACT began organizing meetings among parents from different schools, and it became apparent that the problems experienced by parents at Chavez Elementary also were present in other schools. The problems were systemic, so the parents became united around finding a solution that would change not just one school but the whole educational culture in East San José. They visited successful inner-city schools in Oakland and in New York, and began dreaming about what could be accomplished in San José. Under political pressure from PACT and the parents from

East San José, the school board approved the creation of one charter elementary school and three small autonomous schools. Within three years, three of the four schools started by PACT were, according to standardized testing, achieving the same kind of educational success normally associated with school districts in wealthy, predominantly white, suburbs.

Oddly, the success wasn't welcomed by the school board, which, after a change in administration, started backing away from its former support of small and charter schools, because they feared the creation of a two-tiered system in which resources were taken from mainstream schools and given to higher achieving schools. "We were in a deadlock," Matt explained, "where it was clear that our strategy around these small, autonomous schools really relied on the good will and honest support of the district, and that was not there. The schools were so successful that the district couldn't just close them, so the district found all these other ways just to mess with them."

In response the reformers turned to charter schools, partnering with groups like Rocketship to build excellent schools in the hope that the success of charter schools would encourage and perhaps force the school district to improve the quality of education in their schools as well.

Reflecting on the work of educational reform in East San José, Matt Hammer insists that PACT's role was really minor compared to that of the community members with children in the schools.

> We were able to find and train and connect a large group of immigrants, mostly moms. They themselves moved a system that at some level didn't have to be accountable to them because they weren't voters.
>
> Mainly the efforts to build strong schools were successful because people were working through congregations, so it wasn't just a small group of parents pushing against the school board. It was these big congregations that are full of people, including a lot of voters, and are long-term institutions in the community. And the system felt a need to respond. If it had been just a little group of undocumented moms, they would have gotten way less attention from the system, but because these immigrants sort of linked themselves to these big institutions they were able to leverage the connection to get things done.

Empowering Immigrant Parents

One way or another, Preston Smith, Tom Luschei, and Matt Hammer all mentioned the importance of giving parents a voice in the education of their children, something that often is difficult within immigrant communities. If local school districts are run by elected school boards whose members are responsible to voters, they need not answer to the concerns and demands of nonvoting noncitizens. It's especially problematic when those nonvoting noncitizens are undocumented, but charter schools and other alternative educational institutions can provide those parents with a real voice in their children's educations.

Charter schools like Rocketship and alternative schools like LUCHA only survive when parents choose to send their children to them. The same parents who enroll their children in nontraditional educational institutions also may send their children back into traditional schools, so the teachers and administrators must be attentive to parents' needs. It is an economic necessity that provides parents with direct influence over their children's educational process, and not just within the charter and alternative schools. When traditional schools exist alongside high-quality nontraditional schools, traditional schools are forced to improve if they want to survive, and they too must listen to parents' voices.

It seemed to me that educational reform in East San José was a democratizing process that empowered otherwise marginalized parents, but I wanted to test my assumption. So on the third day of the school year, I met with a woman named Maria Teresa who, like me, has two children enrolled at Rocketship's gleaming new *Sí Se Puede* Academy. Maria Teresa and I have third-grade daughters who have been classmates since kindergarten. I taught her how to make pesto, while she explained the secrets of enchilada sauce to my wife. Maria Teresa and I both have three children, and we both spend a lot of time volunteering at the school. Unlike me, she is undocumented, single and, at the time we met, she had been unemployed for more than a year.

When we met to talk about educational reform, it had been two months since I interviewed Preston Smith. Functioning as the equivalent of a public school superintendent, Preston had worked hard to open the second Rocketship academy on time, and he was successful in his efforts. Maria Teresa and I were impressed with the new facility as we sat down in the cafeteria on tables that hadn't yet seen many hot lunches.

I knew that Maria Teresa's eldest daughter—then an eighth grader—had started out in a traditional school, and I asked Maria Teresa about the difference between being a parent at a regular school and being a parent in the alternative schools born out of the activism of the local faith community.

> I've seen a great difference on this area. In the regular schools the parents were invited to participate, but only so far. There are limits. They don't have a say in the hiring of teachers, for example, like we do at LUCHA or the charter schools. In these new schools, we've been included more as parents.
>
> We're used to how it is in Mexico, where the kids go to school and the teachers are in charge of everything. The parents are in charge of the kids, but only outside of school. In the school the teachers were in control and we were expected to support that. I like the change here. Here you see the schools asking for parental involvement. It's important because the parents have power. If we want to, we can go to another school in a moment, and I think the district sees this. They see that the children are happier in charter schools, and they will do more to help the children in traditional schools.
>
> Here I feel almost as if I am in my house, because here a person is free to give an opinion, to participate. Here I can talk to the teachers, for example, about the reading homework—if it's too hard or not hard enough. Here I can participate in my children's learning, and as a single mother I have the freedom to help.

I said goodbye to Maria Teresa and started walking home through the neighborhood. I greeted Preston Smith, who was on the street, directing traffic and talking to the new school's neighbors, and it struck me that while I suspect there are few inner-city educators better than Preston Smith, the success of the schools he establishes is entirely dependant upon people like Maria Teresa, parents who are willing to help make the schools flourish.

The work of these parents—many of whom, like Maria Teresa, are undocumented—is paying off. The alternative schools in my neighborhood are succeeding, which, in turn, is forcing the traditional public schools to improve. Thanks to Maria Teresa and others like her, my children, though they live in the inner city, are attending some of the best schools in the state of California. If my children succeed academically and are, therefore, able to find meaningful work in life that makes them happy and sustains them economically, I will have a cadre of undocumented mothers, including Maria Teresa, to thank for it.

So, who is my neighbor? The teaching of Jesus, in the parable of the Good Samaritan, suggests that a person's neighbor is the marginalized foreigner who blesses him or her. If that's the case, if Jesus is correct, then Maria Teresa, an undocumented, unemployed, single mother from Mexico is my neighbor.

Reflection and Action

In the seventh chapter of the Gospel of Mark, there is a story in which Jesus is traveling in the southern part of what today we call Lebanon. While staying near the Phoenician city of Tyre, Jesus meets a woman of that country. The woman asks Jesus to heal her daughter, who is possessed by an unclean spirit.

At first, Jesus refuses, citing God's historical preference for the Jewish people, and he does so in a way that is shocking and offensive to most modern readers: "'Let the children be fed first, for it is not fair to take the children's food and throw it to the dogs.'"

Seemingly undaunted by Jesus' canine comparison, the woman answered, "Sir, even the dogs under the table eat the children's crumbs." (Mark 7:28–29)

Jesus relented, and he healed the woman's daughter. In that passage we see a firm affirmation of the idea that the kingdom of God does not recognize national boundaries or ethnic divisions. American Christians are challenged by the story of Jesus' encounter with the Lebanese (then called "Syrophoenician") woman to pray not just for our country but for all countries, If we have the audacity to sing "God Bless America," we must, in our hearts, also ask God to bless other lands and other peoples, for ours is the God of every nation.

For Christians who believe that the kingdom of God is not limited to the United States, the following actions are natural:

1. Get to know your neighbors. Nearly every community in the United States has residents who have immigrated across the U.S./Mexico border. Find the immigrant community and make friends. Often the immigrant population includes folks that go unnoticed: they bus our tables when we are out to eat, they mow our lawns, they clean our houses and workspaces. By their presence they bless us. Go meet them.
2. Find a good independently owned Mexican restaurant. These are often the best places to meet immigrants from Mexico. Ask the wait staff what's good.
3. Go to church. Find a congregation with a large immigrant population and join them for worship. Even if you don't speak Spanish, worshiping with immigrants can be a deeply moving experience.
4. Get involved. In the book's final section I wrote about the work of a few organizations and people who are doing good work among immigrants. These are good organizations and dedicated people, but it is a tiny sampling of the good work happening among immigrants in the United States and elsewhere. Find organizations doing good work in migrant communities. In particular, be on the lookout for groups designed and led by immigrants themselves.
5. If you cannot find individuals and organizations active in immigrant communities, find out what services are needed and find out if the efforts of local churches and nonprofits can be directed to meet those needs.
6. Drink *Café Justo* coffee. No matter where you stand on immigration issues, you may like coffee, and the one issue upon which everyone seems to agree is that the best way to address undocumented immigration is through economic development in Mexico. *Café Justo* provides a good cup of coffee and some calm agreement within the storms of controversy that surround immigration issues. Visit *Café Justo* and treat yourself to some beans: www.justcoffee.org.
7. If you are a member of a faith community, start a conversation around whether or not your congregation can provide sanctuary for someone facing the threat of deportation.
8. Consider visiting the border to learn about the realities of immigration. If you are part of a community of faith, find out if your denomination is doing any good work along the border. If not, check out the programs at Borderlinks, whose work comes highly recommended: www.borderlinks.org.

Conclusion

Mi Beautiful *Barrio*

On December 11 each year it is impossible to find a parking space in my neighborhood. I live across the street from Our Lady of Guadalupe Roman Catholic Church in East San José, a church that increasingly is becoming a place of pilgrimage for Mexican immigrants living in the San Francisco Bay Area. It is the only church in the region that is named for Mexico's patron saint, and it has the distinction of being the congregation in which Cesar Chavez was confirmed and nurtured in the faith.

December 12 is the feast day of Our Lady of Guadalupe, and on the eve of her feast Mexican immigrants converge on my neighborhood in numbers that are hard to imagine. Traffic moves at speeds similar to those endured in shopping mall parking lots on the day after Thanksgiving. My street, which ordinarily is somewhat drab, turns into a Latin American bazaar. Both sidewalks are crammed with stalls selling *churros* and *elotes*, and plaster-of-paris images of *La Virgen Morena*, and *serapes,* and Disney Princess blankets, and roses to commemorate the appearance of the Mother of Heaven to Juan Diego Cuauhtlatoatzin at Tepeyac near Mexico City in 1531.

All night long the faithful keep watch, praying, singing, lighting candles, and dancing. The music is eclectic, reflecting the influence of immigrants from all over Mexico: Aztec drums and mariachi combos share the stage with *rock en Español* bands and the um-pa-pas of polka-inspired *banda* from the Rio Grande valley. The pilgrims find sustenance in the Eucharist and in the street vendors' fare and in tacos cooked and sold by the men of the parish—tacos whose flavor is a reflection of divine favor.

The celebration lasts until first light, when the gathered congregants join their voices in *Las Mañanitas*, the traditional Mexican birthday song: *Que linda está la mañana en que vengo a saludarte / venimos todos con gusto y placer a felicitarte* (How beautiful is the morning in which I come to greet you / with happiness and pleasure we come to wish you joy).

For years, my neighborhood has been a predominantly Hispanic barrio, most of whose residents come from Mexico. It is not a wealthy neighborhood. There are no Starbucks in my neighborhood and no McDonald's. We do have a good supply of excellent taquerias, and there are places to get new tires on your car. Small markets seem to be thriving off the sale of groceries, international phone cards, Tecate beer, and replica Mexican soccer jerseys.

An overwhelming majority of my neighbors speak Spanish, and I suspect that a lot of the people I pass on the street came north from Mexico and other parts of Latin America without proper documents.

The neighborhood is changing, however, as an increasing number of immigrants from Asia find their way into the barrio. Around the corner from my house, and three blocks from Cesar Chavez's childhood home, a small house recently has been converted into a Cambodian Buddhist monastery. From time to time, when the weather is particularly nice, the resident monks can be seen out in the front yard, resplendent in saffron robes, playing bocce ball.

A neighborhood's transformation is inevitable. The human story is one in which some people stay in a place, putting down roots, while others migrate, causing populations to change over time. Such migration is probably good for human communities, but the conflict caused by migration is as old as the first murder, discussed in the introduction to this book. Cain, the farmer and founder of cities, killed his brother, Abel, the nomadic herder—the migrant—in a fit of jealous rage.

The anger of sedentary populations against migrants is rooted in fear—fear that the migrants will consume more than their share of the local resources, fear that an infusion of new ideas and cultural norms will dilute and pollute the comforts of established and rooted communities. The idea that the God who once looked with favor upon the sacrifices of Abel would accept the prayers and supplications of newcomers, that God would respond to their plight with blessings and not with curses, can be terrifying.

Much of the current American response to what often is called an immigration crisis is rooted in the same fear that has inspired America's long history of unjust immigration law. Throughout our history, the demonized immigrant groups have changed (the Irish, the Chinese, the Japanese, the Italians), but the fear has remained constant. Many Americans fear a future in which immigrants compete for American jobs and for America's dwindling educational and health-care resources. We are afraid that newcomers will burden the system without paying taxes, and we are afraid that immigrants will change American culture in fundamental ways, so that English will no longer be a dominant language, or our historical connection to Europe will be replaced with a nostalgia for Mexico or for exotic locales on the far side of the Pacific Rim.

In many ways my neighborhood embodies the future America that so many Americans fear. A person doesn't need to speak Spanish to do business in my barrio, but it helps; the churches worship in Spanish. You're more likely to find salsa than catsup at the corner store; my neighbors like to follow the San Franciso Forty-Niners, but they tend to get more excited about *Las Chivas,* a soccer team from Guadalajara.

I cannot predict the future. I have no idea if my neighborhood is a microcosm of a future American demographic, but I hope it is. There is nothing to fear about the America my barrio represents. We have a graffiti problem and our public schools are subpar, but that's true in almost every urban neighborhood in America. Mostly we are happy, we get along, we love our children, we work hard, and we pay our way. This is a healthy, vibrant community.

American Christians are faced with a choice. We can welcome immigrant strangers, extending hospitality and protection to those who come into our land sincerely seeking a better life, or we can react with fear to the newcomers, allowing that fear to diminish our Christianity and, ultimately, our humanity.

It's an easy choice because, really, we have nothing to fear.

On a particularly fine evening in the late spring of 2008, my family ate dinner out on the patio behind our townhouse in East San José. That night, my foster daughter's best friend was spending the night. Both young women are refugees from Burma, and we were teaching them how to eat artichokes, that most chichi staple of Northern California cuisine.

Next door, in the townhouse with which we share a common wall, a birthday party was in full swing. My good-hearted neighbor—the father of the birthday boy—is a native of Mexico's Sinola state. He first crossed the border illegally in the days before Ronald Reagan granted amnesty to undocumented immigrants in 1986. He's a landscaper by trade and by calling. On the bits of untended common area in our housing complex he has planted *nopales* and jalapeños. On more than one occasion he's coached my Chinese-born daughter in the art of using a mitt to catch a baseball.

And on that warm night in late April, he called my name across the fence that divides us. He had a plate of shrimp for me—*camarones a la diábola*—cooked in a sauce that made my eyes water and my heart sing. The Burmese teenagers at my table were overjoyed. Here was food they understood: it came from the ocean and it was spicy. This was no mutant thistle dipped in the yuppie goofiness of mayonnaise mixed with fresh herbs, crushed pepper, and the juice of a Meyer lemon.

I passed back a homemade baguette. My neighbors received the loaf graciously, and I have no idea if they enjoyed it, though I like to think that someone figured out that French bread dipped in Mexican salsa is a marvelous treat.

This is my neighborhood, and this is the America we are helping to build when we provide sanctuary for God's children whose well-being is threatened by America's misguided immigration policies. It's full of immigrants like my neighbor and my daughters. There's nothing to fear. If this is America's future, we could do a whole lot worse.

Study Questions

*T*he following questions are intended to move individuals or groups toward a greater recognition of migrants as neighbors. Each question corresponds to a chapter in the book.

1. Every American not entirely descended from the people living in the Western Hemisphere before the arrival of Europeans is the product of immigration. What is the story of your family? Why did they leave their homes? Were they fleeing wars and oppression? Were they looking for economic opportunities not available in their homelands? Were they forced to immigrate as slaves or as forced laborers? How does the experience of your family's immigration affect your perception of those who choose to enter the United States without papers today?

2. Whose side is God on? The United States/Mexico border is a place where the world's wealthiest and most powerful nation abuts the developing world. Those who cross the border usually do so for the sake of others—family members and loved ones who are impoverished. Is it possible to imagine illegal entry into the United States as an act of faithfulness?

3. Read the Bible using your imagination to foster an immigrant spirituality. Consider, for example, what may be the best-loved words in Holy Writ:

> The LORD is my shepherd; I shall not want.
> He maketh me to lie down in green pastures:

He leadeth me beside the still waters.
He restoreth my soul:
He leadeth me in paths of righteousness for his name's sake.

Yea, though I walk through the valley of the shadow of death,
I will fear no evil: for thou art with me;
Thy rod and thy staff they comfort me.

Thou preparest a table before me
In the presence of mine enemies:
Thou anointest my head with oil;
My cup runneth over.

Surely goodness and mercy
Shall follow me all the days of my life
And I will dwell in the house of the LORD forever.
(Psalm 23, KJV)

Is it possible to read these familiar words as an undocumented immigrant might? For most Christians the shepherd referenced in this psalm is Jesus, who in John's Gospel referred to himself as "the Good Shepherd" who lays down his life for his sheep (John 10:11–18). May we also think of Jesus as "*El Buen Coyote*" (the Good Coyote) who smuggles people into a land of opportunity? The idea that Jesus is *El Buen Coyote* was first suggested by Bob Ekblad, who works with migrants through Tierra Nueva, a ministry in Burlington, Washington. In *Reading the Bible with the Damned* he writes,

> I've been seeing Jesus more and more as our "Buen Coyote." Jesus crosses us over into the kingdom against the law, by grace. We cannot save ourselves through observing laws. Jesus liberates us, Jesus saves us. He doesn't even charge. He just wants us to trust him and to follow.[1]

How does our understanding of this passage change if we understand that for some people green pastures lie across a heavily guarded international border? What if the still waters to which God leads us are found in the Sonora desert? Can the Valley of the Shadow of Death refer to a remote arroyo, or dry desert wash used by migrants and drug smugglers to elude the United States Border Patrol? (See chapter 8.)

4. The ninth of the Ten Commandments demands that we not "bear false witness against our neighbor" (Exod. 20:16). This is more than a command against simple lying; it is a demand that we bear witness to the truth when we speak about our neighbors. If we assent to the proposition that undocumented immigrants are our neighbors, than what does it mean to tell the truth about those who cross America's borders? How does one respond to the suggestion that undocumented immigrants are criminals who harm the American economy by burdening public services and taking American jobs? How does one respond biblically, factually, and truthfully?

5. What interest do the people of the United States have in preserving the happiness of families? Is it in the national interest to divide families living in the United States, or to prevent parents from earning money that can support their spouses, children, and parents in Mexico?

6. Most of the people sentenced in Judge Brack's courtroom are convicted of felonies for engaging in the pursuit of the same happiness most Americans take for granted. Should the pursuit of happiness—a right most Americans consider to be inalienable and God-ordained—be criminalized, or is the pursuit of happiness a fundamental right? If the pursuit of happiness *is* an inalienable human right, how should America's immigration laws reflect that right?

7. How do your own economic choices affect immigration? Do your habits of consumption and your use of services create jobs that entice people to cross the border at the risk of their lives? When and where do you encounter immigrants as you go about your daily life? How do you know they are immigrants? What kinds of jobs are they doing that, directly or indirectly, impact your life?

8. Does having a fence that stretches across much of the U.S./Mexico border make you feel safer? If so, why?

9. Reflecting upon the experience of the United Church of Christ in Simi Valley, which endured a year of sometimes violent protests in order to provide sanctuary for Liliana, is there anything so important

to you or to your faith community that you (or they) would be willing to endure a year of such protests each Sunday during worship?

10. Reflecting upon the ways in which empowering immigrant parents improves the education of their children, in what other ways may empowering immigrants improve the lives of immigrants and their neighbors?

Notes

CHAPTER 1: FATHER TORIBIO'S GHOST

1. In Mexico, as in all Spanish-speaking countries, a person's family name does not come last. Usually a person's last name is the name of her or his mother. Therefore, in the case of St. Toribio Romo, the last name "González" is only used on the most formal occasions. The name "Romo" is what most Americans would consider to be a last name.

2. Among the many unresolved disputes between the United States and Mexico is the name for the body of water that marks the border between El Paso, Texas and the Gulf of Mexico, a river that has inspired artists as diverse as Cormac McCarthy and Duran Duran. In the United States we call it the Rio Grande. In Mexico it is *El Rio Bravo.*

3. Tiberio Munari, *Santo Toribio Romo: Sacerdote y Mártir de Jesucristo,* 8th edition (Guadalajara: Ediciones Xaverianas, 2007), 23.

4. Ibid., 29.

5. This prayer comes from the reverse side of a prayer card depicting the face of St. Toribio Romo that I purchased at the Guadalupe bookstore in the eastside of San José, CA. No publication information is given.

6. For a particularly compelling examination of the spirituality of immigration, see Daniel G. Groody, "Jesus and the Undocumented Immigrant: A Spiritual Geography of a Crucified People," *Theological Studies*, vol. 70, no. 2, 298.

7. No publication information is printed in the *Novena* booklet, which is titled *Novena en Honor a Santo Toribio Romo.*

8. Bill Minkel is a first order Franciscan, a fully ordained Roman Catholic priest, but he prefers to be called "Brother" rather than "Father."

CHAPTER 2: IMMIGRATION AS A BIBLICAL JOURNEY

1. Samuel Kobia, opening sermon at Thanksgiving worship, World Council of Churches, http://www.oikoumene.org/en/resources/documents/general-secretary/sermons/and-who-is-my-neighbour.html.

2. Much of what I know about the rabbinical community at Jamnia comes from the book *Christianity and Rabbinic Judaism: A Parallel History of Their Origins and Early Development*, ed. Hershel Shanks (Washington, D.C.: Biblical Archaeology Society, 1992). In particular I have drawn from articles in the book written by Lee I. A. Levine ("Judaism from the Destruction of Jerusalem to the End of the Second Jewish Revolt") and by James Charlesworth ("Christians and Jews in the First Six Centuries").

3. The rabbis at Jamnia didn't invent the idea that a corpus of writings should be considered sacred; rather they chose among various collections of books already in use throughout the Jewish world. Among the more controversial and interesting inclusions was the book of Esther, which makes no mention of God, but which does provide a strong narrative about living faithfully as an immigrant community.

4. Biblical scholars generally agree that Mark is the oldest of the three Synoptic Gospels and that the authors of Matthew and Luke borrowed from Mark while writing their Gospels.

CHAPTER 3: IMMIGRATION IN CHURCH HISTORY

1. Peter C. Phan, "Migration in the Patristic Era," in *A Promised Land, a Perilous Journey: Theological Reflections on Migration*, ed. Daniel G. Groody and Gioacchino Campese (Notre Dame, IN: University of Notre Dame Press, 2008), 49.

2. *Early Christian Fathers*, trans. and ed. Cyril C. Richardson (Philadelphia: Westminster Press, 1953), 43.

3. Ibid., 131.

4. I am indebted to Peter Phan's essay for exposing me to the immigrant spirituality found in the work of the Church Fathers.

5. *Early Christian Fathers*, 217.

6. Seriously, this is a real brand of beer. I recommend it.

7. To assert that Geneva was tolerant compared to the rest of Europe in the middle of the sixteenth century isn't saying much. John Calvin and his followers insisted on a strict adherence to Calvinist doctrine, but compared to the Inquisition, the Calvinists were gentle and open-minded.

8. Alister McGrath, *A Life of John Calvin* (Oxford: Basil Blackwell, 1990), 121.

9. The vertical expansion of Geneva's skyline for the accommodation of foreign refugees is the subject of a particularly compelling exhibit at *La Musée International de la Réforme* in Geneva.

10. Banking and watch-making are more profitable than diplomacy, but international organizations and NGOs are the largest employers in Geneva.

11. Williston Walker, *John Calvin: The Organizer of Reformed Protestantism (1509–1564)* (New York: Schocken Books, 1969), 313.

12. Hugh Young Reyburn, *John Calvin: His Life, Letters, and Work* (London: Hodder and Stoughton, 1914), 161.

13. John Calvin is often and incorrectly remembered as a theocratic dictator in Geneva. Calvin was the head of the Genevan church, but he never held political office. He was a man of prominence and influence in his community who tried to sway the city, and when Calvin's allies controlled the city council, Calvin usually

got his way. For much of his time in Geneva, however, Calvin's agenda was frustrated by a skeptical and reluctant city government. This may have been wise governance on the part of the city council; Theodore Beza, Calvin's successor as head of the Genevan church, reports that Calvin's detractors were to be blamed for the great reformer's stress-induced hemorrhoids.

14. Theodore Beza, *The Life of John Calvin* (Faverdale, UK: Evangelical Press, 1997), 105.

15. Bill Bryson, *Made in America* (London: Minerva, 1994), 5.

16. *Webster's Ninth New Collegiate Dictionary* (Springfield, MA: Merriam-Webster, Inc., 1984).

17. Bryson, *Made in America*, 4.

18. M. Daniel Carroll R., *Christians at the Border: Immigration, the Church, and the Bible* (Grand Rapids: Baker Books, 2008), 61.

19. Pope John Paul II, "The Church and Illegal Immigration: Annual Message for World Migration Day 1996 given July 25, 1995," http://www.vatican.va/holy_father/john_paul_ii/messages/migration/documents/hf_jp-ii_mes_25071995_undocumented_migrants_en.html.

20. CatholicHistory.net, "Spotlight: Catholic Immigration," http://www.catholichistory.net/Spotlights/SpotlightImmigration.htm.

21. Bryson, *Made in America*, 176.

22. Robert Louis Stevenson, *Kidnapped* (New York: Grosset & Dunlap, 1948), 161–62.

CHAPTER 4: ON RENDERING TO CAESAR AND GOD

1. Robert McAfee Brown, *Saying Yes and Saying No: On Rendering to God and Caesar* (Philadelphia: Westminster Press, 1986), 90.

2. A similar fate befell Iraqis displaced by war after the fall of Saddam Hussein.

3. Hubert Herring, *A History of Latin America,* 3rd edition (New York: Alfred A. Knopf, 1968), 312–13.

4. Edwardo Porter, "Illegal Immigrants Are Bolstering Social Security with Billions." *New York Times*, April 5, 2005.

CHAPTER 5: ZOE LOFGREN AND THE POLITICS OF IMMIGRATION REFORM

1. Wendell Berry, "A Citizen's Response to the National Security Strategy of the United States of America," in *Citizen's Dissent: Security, Morality, and Leadership in an Age of Terror*, Wendell Berry and David James Duncan (Great Barrington, MA: The Orion Society, 2003), 14.

2. Congress of the United States Congressional Budget Office, *Immigration Policy in the United States* (February, 2006), 9.

3. While immigrants from all nations were technically welcome in the United States, no one who wasn't free, white, and male was allowed to become a naturalized citizen after 1790. So although Asians, blacks, and other minority groups could technically come to America, they had restricted rights as far as voting, holding property, and testifying in court were concerned.

4. Bryson, *Made in America*, 162–63.

5. The full text of the Page Act can be found online at "Page Act of 1875," 43rd Congr., 2nd sess., http://w3.uchastings.edu/wingate/pageact.htm.

6. Kerry Abrams, "Polygamy, Prostitution, and the Federalization of Immigration Law," *Columbia Law Review* 105, no. 3 (April 2005): 641; available at SSRN:http://ssrn.com/abstract=854045.

7. Ibid.

8. A text of the Chinese Exclusion Act of 1882 can be found at Our Documents, "Transcript of Chinese Exclusion Act (1882)," http://www.ourdocuments.gov/doc.php?flash=false&doc=47&page=transcript.

9. University of Washington–Bothell, "1917 Immigration Act," US Immigration Online, http://library.uwb.edu/guides/USimmigration/1917_immigration_act.html.

10. U.S. Department of State, "The Immigration Act of 1924 (The Johnson-Reed Act)," U.S. Department of State, http://www.state.gov/r/pa/ho/time/id/87718.htm.

11. U.S. Department of State, "The Immigration and Nationality Act of 1952 (The McCarran-Walter Act)," U.S. Department of State, http://www.state.gov/r/pa/ho/time/cwr/87719.htm.

12. Center for Immigration Studies, "Three Decades of Mass Immigration: The Legacy of the 1965 Immigration Act," Center for Immigration Studies, September 1995, http://www.cis.org/articles/1995/back395.html.

13. Matt S. Meier and Feliciano Rivera, *The Chicanos: A History of Mexican Americans* (New York: Hill and Wang, 1972), 115–49.

14. Ibid., 144.

15. Ibid., 160–63.

16. In Spanish the word *"bracero"* refers to someone who works with his arms ("*brazo*" means "arm").

17. Gilbert Paul Carrasco, "Latinos in the United States: Invitation and Exile," in Juan F. Parea, ed., *Immigrants Out! The New Nativism and the Anti-Immigrant Impulse in the United States* (New York: New York University Press, 1997), 197.

18. Zoe Lofgren, "Rep. Lofgren Releases Statement in Response to White House Immigration Meeting," U.S. House of Representatives, June 25, 2009, http://www.lofgren.house.gov/index.php?option=com_content&task=view&id=546&Itemid=89.

CHAPTER 6: THE BUSIEST (AND KINDEST) FEDERAL JUDGE IN AMERICA

1. Jack Kemp, "Immigration Reform Will Help Keep This Nation Strong," HumanEvents.com, July 18, 2006, http://www.humanevents.com/article.php?id=16091. I am grateful to Frank Schaeffer for sharing this quote with me as an illustration that one needs not be politically progressive to be pro-immigrant. The story of my meeting with Judge Brack proves Frank right.

2. Russell Goldman, "What's Clogging the Courts? Ask America's Busiest Judge," ABC News.com, July 23, 2008, http://abcnews.go.com/TheLaw/Story?id=5429227.

3. To read the text of the Kennedy-McCain immigration reform bill, see *Comprehensive Immigration Reform Act of 2007*, S. 1348, 110th Cong., 1st sess., http://thomas.loc.gov/cgi-bin/query/z?c110:S1348: A summary of the bill can be found at Crystal Patterson, "Quick Guide to Kennedy-McCain Immigration Bill," Daily Kos, May 13, 2005, http://www.dailykos.com/story/2005/5/13/112653/285.

4. To be fair, the only bit of Judge Brack's judicial record that I could find was a decision in which he refused to find that the depictions of crosses on the seal of the city of Las Cruces, New Mexico, was a violation of the First Amendment's disestablishment clause. It's likely that Judge Brack's decision in this case had less to do with conservative inclinations than with a working knowledge of basic Spanish. In Spanish "Las Cruces" means "The Crosses."

CHAPTER 7: *FRONTERA DE CRISTO*

1. Gustavo Gutiérrez, *A Theology of Liberation* (Maryknoll, New York:, Orbis Books, 1973), 145.

2. My apologies to William Butler Yeats.

3. Entering Mexico from the United States is no problem. The border guards there seldom check papers, and only check cars randomly. This is changing, but for now the border south is totally open. A person can walk or ride a bike across the border with no difficulty, as this man did.

4. Karen Tumlin, Linton Joaquin, and Ranjana Natarajan, *A Broken System: Confidential Reports Reveal Failures in U.S. Detention Centers* (Los Angeles: National Immigration Law Center, 2009), xii.

5. The story of *Café Justo* is told in the book *Just Coffee: Caffeine with a Conscience* by Mark Adams and Tommy Bassett III (Douglas, AZ: Just Trade Center, 2009).

CHAPTER 8: WATER IN THE DESERT

1. CRREDA stands for "*Centro de Rehabilitación y Recuperación para Enfermos de Drogadicción y Alcoholismo*" which, in English translates as "Center for Rehabilitation and Recovery for Those Sick with Drug Addiction and Alcoholism."

2. Nancy Rytina and John Simanski, "Apprehensions by the U.S. Border Patrol: 2005–2008." *Fact Sheet*, Department of Homeland Security Office of Immigration Statistics, June 2009.

3. *Illegal Immigration: Border-Crossing Deaths Have Doubled Since 1995; Border Patrol's Efforts to Prevent Deaths Have Not Been Fully Evaluated*, GAO, August 2006.

4. Coalición de Derechos Humanos, "Arizona Recovered Remains," January 23, 2007, http://www.derechoshumanosaz.net/index.php?option=com_content&task=view&id=20&Itemid=34.

5. Ashley Powers, "Arizona Immigration Debate at Heart of Littering Case," *Los Angeles Times*, August 13, 2009.

6. The Gadsden Purchase was a second purchase a few years after the end of the Mexican-American War. The United States bought parts of New Mexico and Arizona from Mexico for the purpose of building a railroad. Many Mexicans felt betrayed

by their government for capitulating to the United States at the time of the Gadsden Purchase.

7. George W. Bush, "President Bush signs Secure Fence Act," Office of the Press Secretary, October 26, 2006, http://georgewbush-whitehouse.archives.gov/news/releases/2006/10/20061026.html.

8. Updated maps of the fence's progress can be downloaded at Center for Border Patrol, "Border Security," U.S. Department of Homeland Security, http://www.cbp.gov/xp/cgov/border_security/.

CHAPTER 9: LILIANA AND THE NEW SANCTUARY MOVEMENT

1. Southern Poverty Law Center, "The Nativists," Intelligence Report, Winter 2005, http://www.splcenter.org/intel/intelreport/article.jsp?pid=980.

2. Marcus, "Minutemen Provoke, Pepper spray, in Simi Valley," Los Angeles Independent Media Center, September 18, 2007, http://la.indymedia.org/news/2007/09/207304.php.

3. Jamiel Shaw, a Los Angeles youth, was murdered in a racially charged, gang-related homicide on March 2, 2008.

4. Digger, "Illegal Alien Liliana Still in Church—One Year Rally Protest—July 27," Diggers Realm, http://www.diggersrealm.com/mt/archives/002866.html.

5. Clergy and Laity United for Economic Justice, "About Clue," http://www.clueca.org/1-about-us.htm.

6. Emily Bazar, "Illegal Immigrants Find Refuge in Holy Places," *USA Today*, July 7, 2007.

CHAPTER 10: GOOD *ESCUELAS EN LA* 'HOOD: IMMIGRANTS AND SCHOOL

1. Gary Natriello, Edward L. McDill, and Aaron M. Pallas, *Schooling Disadvantaged Children: Racing against Catastrophe* (New York: Teachers College Press, 1990).

2. Rocketship Education, "Contact Us," http://www.rsed.org/about.html.

3. Cesar Chavez Elementary School is named after the school's most famous alumnus; Cesar Chavez grew up in the neighborhood. He was introduced to a radicalized, progressive Catholicism at Our Lady of Guadalupe, where he was confirmed.

STUDY QUESTIONS

1. Bob Ekblad, *Reading the Bible with the Damned* (Louisville, KY: Westminster John Knox Press, 2005), 182.

Index